LAND ALIVE

LAND ALIVE

THE WORLD OF NATURE
AT ONE FAMILY'S DOOR

RONALD N. ROOD

Drawings by Edward J. Brundage

THE STEPHEN GREENE PRESS

BRATTLEBORO, VERMONT · 1962

ACKNOWLEDGMENTS

I wish to thank the National Audubon Society for permission to include "Pokey," which appeared originally in *Audubon Magazine*. I am grateful also to the editors of *Reader's Digest* for permission to quote from the article on bluebirds (Copyright 1962 by The Reader's Digest Association, Inc.) by Robert Gannon. Bruno Schmidt of the Department of Geology of Middlebury College was of much help with the chapter titled "Ice Out!" I'd like to thank Mrs. Patty Hier, as well, for being such a patient and understanding typist.

I am grateful for the plant and animal neighbors who share my hundred acres—and to Peg and the children for helping me appreciate them. R.N.R.

Second Printing

The earth is the Lord's, and the fulness thereof;

the world, and they that dwell therein.

PSALM XXIV:I

CONTENTS

Foreword

ONE DAY last summer we were seated on the shady lawn at Betty Douglas's house. Betty is one of the best cooks anywhere. People take the ferry across Lake Champlain from New York State to Shoreham just to get her home cooking.

A Pennsylvania car pulled up beside her display case with its bread and pastries. "What kind of cake is that?" the driver wanted to know.

"Maple sugar cake," said Betty.

I wasn't prepared for the next question. "We've been all over Vermont these last few days," said our visitor, "and it seems as if everything was maple. Maple fudge, maple syrup, maple sugar. Where does it all come from? What does a maple tree *look* like, anyway?"

I glanced up at the green canopy above me. Maple. I looked

1

at the next tree. It, too, was maple. In fact, every one of the trees on this cool Vermont lawn was a good sugar maple, the source of the very frosting on the cake.

Betty introduced the trees and the visitor to each other. Almost in wonder, he went over and felt of the rough, gray bark. "Well, what do you know? I'm looking all over Vermont for maple trees and they're all around me!"

He bought the cake and took it to the car. We could see him gesturing toward the trees as he showed the frosting to his children. When they drove off they were still looking back in awe.

I know just how they felt. The same thing has happened to me many times. Not with sugar maple, perhaps, for I can't remember when I didn't know this grand old tree, but with so many other things around me.

I recall the revelation when I learned that the hot water you draw for your shower originally flowed cool and dark in a woodland brook. I remember my conversion when I saw rough, grimy logs turn into gleaming wooden boards at a sawmill. Up until then, it had happened only in my schoolbooks and I hadn't really believed it.

Nor will I forget the remark of my city nephew who happened to visit us one time just after a hog had been killed. The carcass hung in the barn, head and feet still attached but the hair taken off. He took one look and ran back out to his father, who was still in the car.

"Look, Daddy!" he pointed excitedly. "A pig—made out of meat!"

Just as the "meat" is hidden in the living pig and the boards are hidden in the growing tree, there are many other surprises in the commonplace. Stop your car along a country road sometime. Or better still, take a genuine muscular, arm-swinging walk. Your eyes, ears and nose tell you a host of stories that are hidden to the man in the automobile.

You may hear a tree cricket on your walk as it calls the temperature. You may hear a turtle whisper, a frog hum or an ant squeak. Your nose may bring the nostalgic perfume of a faraway skunk—wholly different from the repugnant smell that comes in through your car windows at sixty miles per hour.

Go into the woods and just sit there. Drift in a rowboat without a motor. Lie on your stomach and peer into the grass. Or lie on your back and look at the clouds. Your senses will tell you about a world you only half suspected.

This book is a story of that world. A fragment of it is found on my hundred acres in Vermont. As the seasons move, it reveals itself as a land alive.

WINTER

CHAPTER ONE

Mustela's Visit

"DADDY, does a muskrat ever look like a dachshund?"

I considered that one for a moment. "No, Roger. I guess not. Why?"

"Well, maybe this isn't a muskrat, then. It doesn't look like any of our beavers, either. Anyway it's too small."

My curiosity aroused, I walked over to the window. The landscape was white and the Vermont mountains were lost in a snow flurry. I followed my nine-year-old's gaze to the New Haven River which runs in front of our house.

"Right down there," he said. "Whatever it is just went into that pile of rocks under the bridge."

"Stray cat," I thought to myself. We often saw our neighbor's tabbies out in the fields after mice. I couldn't imagine what a cat would be doing away from home in this snowstorm.

My thoughts were cut short a moment later. Out of the pile of rocks poked a head the size of a small fist. It was followed by a slender black body two feet long.

"Mink, Roger!" I breathed. "A real wild mink. Right in our front yard." I spoke in a hush, even though the windows were closed and the wind rattled the alders.

Now our front yard had afforded nearly every animal the Green Mountains had to offer. Last fall we watched a she-bear and her twin cubs as they poked along on the hillside opposite our home, looking for wild apples. Three years ago we trained our binoculars on a magnificent buck deer as he cavorted in the pasture with our neighbor's horses across the river. The children once brought in a half-grown cottontail rabbit which they had taken away from a weasel on the riverbank. Alison had fed chipmunks out of her hand, and had coaxed a red squirrel to where it nibbled at her shoe. And we had a porcupine in front of our house all one summer, though it really doesn't count because he was a pet. But none of us had ever seen a mink in our front yard before.

He bounced along the river edge as if he were on springs. Unhurried but quick, he investigated every brush-clump, every overhanging stone. Through the binoculars we could see his beady black eyes, his eight-inch furry tail. We even caught a hint of the partial webbing between his toes, for a mink is a creature as much of water as of land.

We watched as he poked with deadly intentness into the base of each clump of brush along the river. Predator that he was, and lord of his own little world, he had little to fear from possible enemies. I contrasted this with the watchful, ready-to-fly attitude of the birds on the feeding tray at that very moment. Although he remained alert to his surroundings, the mink went his way surely, confidently, for few creatures smaller than a dog would face his white teeth. The birds, however, crouched at every movement in the trees. Each shadow might be any of a dozen enemies, ready to strike. The eyes of the mink and other predators, set for straightforward vision, see potential prey; the eyes of songbirds and the host of small rodents are set to the side of the head for a sweeping lookout for danger.

"What's he looking for?" asked Roger.

As if in answer, the mink drew itself erect. Its back arched like that of a slender cat, but with its front paws against its chest. Its luxuriant fur rippled as it poised above a clump of grass. The next instant it lanced forward in a strike. It disappeared in a blinding flurry of snow.

Out of the melee jumped the gray form of a mouse. A split second behind it came the mink, but the mouse's lead was enough. It bounded beneath an overhanging stone.

Then we marked another trait of predators. I had seen it in a pigeon hawk after a bobolink and a bass after a sunfish. Now I saw it again in a mink after a mouse. Unrelenting as they are, they seem to bear no grudge against their prey. Where we'd consider the personality of the mouse or snake—if even for a brief second before killing it with a stick—the predator seems to regard it as only a source of food. Once the hunted is safely away, the hunter goes on about his business. The mink, coming up short against the stone, turned calmly aside.

I have recently read a best-selling novel about a man who spent his entire lifetime trying to "get even" with someone who had cheated him as a child. Such a thing, I believe, is unthinkable in a world where beasts behave like beasts and not like men.

A few years ago I visited a mink farm. The air had been musky with the scent of these animals who share the same family tree as the skunk, the weasel and the otter. Their eyes, showing not the raptor so much as the refugee, followed us as we walked among them. Many of the cages showed worn spots where the little creatures with the valuable fur had bounded, bounded, bounded back and forth next to the wire.

"That's the way they get their exercise," my host had told me.

How different had those hundreds of cooped-up ones been from the lithe hunter before us! There was something unminklike about our front-yard visitor, but none of us thought about it until later. Alison had pulled my natural history off the shelf and was busy studying about *Mustela vison*. "What does 'nocturnal' mean?" she asked. When we explained that it meant "active at night," she chuckled. "If that means he sleeps during the day, our mink must have had insomnia."

Had it been late February or March, we might have understood Mustela's upside-down day, because then he might have been seeking a female for that quick alliance of two wanderers necessary for the continuance of the species. Or had it been among the cowslips of May or the buttercups of June, and the mink a third smaller, there would have been a different reason. Then it would have been a female, driven by the demands of four or five helpless nursing kits in a riverbank den.

But it was only December. This underlined another thing about wild animals. "You can generalize, but you cannot specifize," my forestry professor used to say. For here was our nocturnal mink, unconcernedly abroad in daylight. Thus my hundred acres is always interesting—its inhabitants are never quite predictable. I remember a woodchuck I once saw in a tree, and a ruffed grouse that made friends with one of our chickens. Neither of these things should have happened—but you can't "specifize."

The mink passed upriver and out of sight. We hurried into our coats and ran out on the wooden bridge. The snow crunched under our feet. It made a hollow sound as my wife and I walked carefully on the planks.

We strained our eyes into the snowstorm. Suddenly Peg clutched my arm. "See him?" she hissed.

Mustela had bounded across the ice and was on his way back down the river. In a few moments he'd be directly beneath us.

Now the binoculars brought him to what seemed scarcely a yard away. We saw the soft fur with its longer guard hairs, thickened and primed by the cold artistry of winter. The rounded ears, almost hidden in the fur, somehow reminded me of two radar scoops, alert to the slightest sound. We could see his four claws—curved, sharp as a cat's, but unretractable. I guessed him to weigh close to four pounds—certainly one of the most magnificent specimens I'd seen.

As he came closer, we held our breath. There was a giant boulder at the water's edge. The river, swirling around its tip, was yet unfrozen. The water raced, black and cold, for some ten feet before it again disappeared under the snow and ice. The mink had his choice: scramble up the side of the boulder or go out on the ice in midstream, around the patch of open water.

He did neither, of course. Pausing for a moment at the edge of that pool, he gazed around. He cocked his head and gave us a long, steady look. Then, with a motion so quick that we scarcely saw him go, he disappeared into that frigid torrent.

We waited for what must have been five minutes. The next

11

closest patch of open water was fully a hundred feet downstream. Perhaps his black head surfaced in it for a moment and
was gone again before we saw it. Or perhaps he swam along
under the ice as beavers do, breathing air bubbles trapped on
its underside. At any rate, we never saw him again.

We turned back toward the house. I guess we were both
thinking of that grace, that wildness, and the calmness in the
steady look just before our visitor disappeared.

Peg slipped her arm through mine.

"You know, there's nothing that needs a mink coat," she
said, "as much as a mink."

CHAPTER TWO

Black-Cap

HE LAY upside down in my hand, his black feet clutching my finger. Not a one of my nature books said anything about a bird's facial expression, but this one had a clear look of defiance.

"I'd show *you* if you didn't squeeze me so tight!" it said. I reached over with my left hand to stroke the black-capped head, and got pecked for my pains.

Tom set his Latin book aside. "How'd you ever catch him, Dad?"

I told him, but he could have guessed anyway. This latest

captive, *Parus atricapillus,* whose name was almost as big as he was, had flown into our sun porch that midwinter day. Now he was unable to get out. Better known as the black-capped chickadee, he was the third one we'd caught this season. Our porch is a regular chickadee trap.

Of course, to anyone who knows birds, this is no surprise. Our little gray-and-white mites with the snub-beaks, black caps and bibs will go almost anywhere. They've come in the open window to a dish of sunflower seeds on my table. Sometimes they get caught in between the windows and the storm sash, where they've chased after flies. We found one in our car after a football game. And a favorite feeder in our yard is a cocoanut shell which has been hollowed out, with a hole just big enough for a chickadee. One goes in, clear out of sight, and flies out again with a sunflower seed.

We used sunflower seeds by the twenty-pound lots. "They're wonderful chickadee-bait," my father had once told me. At the time we were sitting in our back yard while four or five of the half-ounce creatures landed on us at once, seeking the seeds he held in his lap. More would have landed if they weren't such individualists. They squabble constantly as to who's going to get the next handout. So they spend part of their time chasing each other away.

Now Alison held our latest captive while I clamped a band around his leg. Thus if we had to rescue him a second time, we'd recognize him. When we let him go he flew to a branch of our sugar maple and busied himself trying to pick the band off. But it held, and two minutes later he had forgotten about it. Soon he was taking his turn at the cocoanut shell.

It was spring: or so said Parus from a dozen different perches in our front yard. Although we hadn't yet torn February off the calendar, and the ice in the river still thickened, the chickadees are inveterate optimists. They whistled the clear, high two-note song they compose specially for spring. Hearing it has been such a welcome relief after the long winter that farmers and lumbermen—who are not on record as a group as caring much about birds—have given this call a name. "Spring Soon," they say, imitating the birds with their voices.

Spring Soon is one of the most easily mimicked of all bird calls. Whistle the highest note you can. Hold it for about two seconds. Then drop down two tones and whistle again for one second. That's all there is to it.

Try it some time where the chickadees are found. In a few minutes you'll have them flitting around your head. Or try kissing the back of your hand loudly. It has much the same effect. Parus is just a feathered question mark. Any unusual sound will bring him in a hurry.

The chickadee is Maine's state bird. But we've seen it along with cardinals and tufted titmice in Raleigh, North Carolina. A flock of them was busy over our picnic table in the Sierras. Several accompanied me as I picked berries north of Fairbanks, Alaska. This little bird, whose better-known call of "chick-a-dee" sounds like its name, covers most of North America. Probably more people know the black-capped chickadee than any other resident American bird. Even in our frozen Vermont, it's with us every month of the year—something which is not attempted by its runner-up for popularity, the robin.

How it manages to keep the tiny spark of existence so brightly fanned through the crackling cold is one of the miracles of nature. Once I read that a chickadee's heart beats some 700 times a minute. This is so fast that the beats cannot be distinguished. An electronic "ear" records the pulse as a low-pitched, steady buzz as it courses the blood through several miles of arteries, veins and capillaries packed into that tiny body. Thus every bit of him is bathed constantly in a stream of blood at some 100 degrees Fahrenheit.

But this same flood of warmth would jell in an instant if it were not for the magic of air. For the very air which carries the cold to every corner of my hundred acres serves as a bird's cushion of life. Trapped in the millions of spaces between the barbs of the feathers, it's an astounding insulation. Within the space of perhaps a quarter-inch of fluffed-out feathers, the air temperature may go from 30 below to 100 above.

Eskimos use bird skins for clothing. I heard of an old farm-house which had goose feathers in its walls as insulation. I've seen sleeping birds on a branch under a January moon, their bodies so perfectly insulated that a puff of snow may remain on their backs all night without melting.

"Spring Soon," call Parus and his flock-mates again. Their hourglass, or season-glass, is more accurate than my calendar. It needs no adjusting one year in four. It is the earth itself, whirling on its orbit, getting a little more light each day as it slants ponderously toward the sun. Increasing day-length, or "photoperiod," as science calls it, molds the flocks of geese into great cackling V's as they strike north. It swells the buds of the pussy willows while their roots stand in the yet frozen earth. And it stirs a song in the chickadee.

It calls forth a reaction in other creatures, too. This fact hit us with a bang—literally and figuratively—a few weeks later. I was helping Fletcher Brown hang his buckets in preparation for sugaring, the season when the maple sap runs fastest and the sweet stuff is collected and boiled down into syrup.

Suddenly a sound ripped the air like a machine gun. We spun around toward it. Again it sounded. Then Fletcher grinned.

"Those hammerheaded woodpeckers!" he said. "Now they're drilling on my sugar buckets."

Woodpeckers have little in the way of a voice but a loud, piercing shriek. It must be jarring even to a lady woodpecker. So, urged by the stirring of spring, they whack a tattoo on a hollow stub. Usually it's high in a tree, but when man nicely provides resounding metal buckets, they're quick to put them to use.

Not all the woodpeckers announced their intentions on Fletcher's metallic bulletin board, or the din would have been hideous. "I wonder," he said one day, "do those males who double in brass get their pick of the ladies?"

The question will never be answered—at least not in our woods or Fletcher's. For these two adjoining chunks of forest now have plastic tubing stretched from tree to tree in the spring. The sap flows through it to collecting tanks and thence goes to the sugarhouse. The galvanized bucket—and the galvanizing racket—are becoming a thing of the past.

By mid-May, the chickadees seldom visited our bird feeders. Now they were busy with household duties. To our delight, a pair took up lodging in an old tree-stub behind our house. In a hole begun by a woodpecker, and further refined by two short little bills, they set up housekeeping.

Nearly everything went into that nest. Grass from the lawnmower, moss from the side of our stone-walled spring, yarn that Peg hung out in short lengths. But the experience of a friend of mine shows what a resourceful little sprite the blackcap can be.

"One of my prize possessions," he recalled to me one day, "was a hat I brought back from Bavaria after the war. It had a real Tyrolean flourish, topped off by a long feather. At the base of the feather were smaller downy ones.

"One day I drove into the yard. The children were having a softball game. I threw my hat and coat aside and joined them. I didn't remember them again until several hours later.

"When I went back out to get them, I saw a chickadee having a tussle with my hat. The little thief had stolen two of the little feathers. As I got there, he gave a tug and got away with the third."

We looked into our own black-cap nest with a flashlight one day when the parents were away. We could just make out five white eggs, about as big as beans, with brownish dots. Some other whitish objects I recognized as feathers from our own henyard. At one side was a naked mass of bluish-pink. As I tapped on the edge of the hole, it jerked upright. Then it resolved itself into a wide-open mouth swaying voicelessly. One little fellow, hatched earlier than the rest, was already looking for dinner.

Quietly I backed down the ladder and walked away, but not before the plucky little parents discovered me. One, its mouth full of flies for the new baby, gobbled down the meal it had brought. Then they dived at me together, chattering and hissing until they had safely vanquished the ladder and me to the door of the barn.

"I think the chickadees are mad at you," the children told me as we watched in vain for them to come after the sunflower seeds the next day. They certainly seemed aloof. Not a seed did they take. Hour after hour they flew back and forth to the hole in the stub, never once noticing the seeds below.

Each time one flew to the hole, we saw that it had a green caterpillar or a mouthful of smaller insects. Then we understood. Those six frantically growing bodies needed protein, not the oil of a seed. Studies have shown that a baby bird may consume more than its weight each day in food. What a mass of insects must have taken the one-way trip through that hole!

Often, when the parents came out again, they had something in their beaks. I suspected it to be the waste from the babies, and the idea repelled me. One day a few yards from the nest they dropped it on a pile of leaves I had raked on the lawn.

Then I saw that it was quite different from what I thought it would be. Waste though it was, it was a perfect little package. Coated with glistening mucus, it was no more dirty than the empty eggshells which the parents had dropped a few days before. So a question which had bothered me from childhood was answered: waste disposal is simple, efficient, and by means of clean little bundles.

For nearly three weeks the parents kept up the grind. From dawn to nightfall they flew in and out of the hole. We could hear the chorus that greeted them as the little birds grew stronger and more demanding. The parents, frayed and soiled, scarcely seemed to find time to catch their own food.

One day a black-capped head appeared at the hole while the parents were away. In a moment it was replaced by another. On the following day they left the nest. We thought they were gone for good. None of us had seen them go.

"Well, they'll be back next winter," I consoled myself the next morning. But then I glanced up at the clothesline. There they were—six chickadees in a row. They sat there, tailless and teetering, sparkling new in their black-and-white suits with the buffy sides. A little apart from them, in her faded gray work clothes sat the mother, seeming only about three fourths their size.

Now I could see how hard she had worked as I compared her to her overstuffed offspring. And the difficulty of being a chickadee came to me further as I looked in vain for her spouse. Caught perhaps by a lucky sweep of a hawk or owl, he never appeared again. But I didn't begrudge the hawk too much. I knew that it, too, had hungry mouths to feed.

I fed my chickadee family all summer and fall. Their tails grew long, and their colors dulled a bit. Finally I could no longer tell them from the twenty or so at my feeding station. Now winter is here as I write these particular words. But already the sun is swinging farther northward.

Any day now, as I watch Parus swing unconcernedly upside down on the end of a twig, I may hear the welcome call, Spring Soon. Then the life of my little black-caps will have come full circle.

CHAPTER THREE

Stories in the Snow

THERE was something wandering around outside. We had heard vague stirrings at night, and twice Jack had run out, all abristle and barking. But we had seen nothing.

Then one midnight Peg jabbed me in the ribs. "Something's walking around in the snow," she whispered.

"One of the horses," I grunted. "Go back to sleep."

I vaguely recall her going to the window to look. We have a couple of saddle horses which have been retired to our pasture from greener fields. We had left them out overnight for exercise. The fence is only fifty feet from our window. Probably it was their footsteps she'd heard in the crusty snow, I told myself.

We thought nothing more about it until after breakfast. Peg went out to get Jack's dish from the back porch. She came back smiling.

"You know that chunk of caraway rye bread that Jack wouldn't touch?" she asked. "Well, it's gone. I suppose a 'horse' got out and ate it last night."

"Of course not. Jack just got hungry, that's all."

"Jack, Dearie, was in the house all night."

Two days later we went to a basketball game. As we returned the frost was settling out of the air. Peg opened the back door to look at the thermometer.

"Br-r-r-r!" she said. "It's nearly ten degrees below . . ."

Her voice trailed away and she beckoned to me.

"I just saw it," she said, as I peered out the door. "It was whitish. And it went up the hill like a big rubber ball. See— there're its tracks."

Two pad marks about the size of playing cards showed in the light frost. They were side by side and about five inches apart. Between them were two smaller prints. The pattern was repeated six feet further along.

Our mystery visitor was a stranger no longer, but the snowshoe hare—possessor of one of nature's finest winter outfits.

Those card-sized prints were of his great hind feet, placed ahead of the smaller forefeet as he doubled himself in his leaps over the snow. Although he weighs less than five pounds as a rule, such is the spring in those legs that he's been known to cover ten feet at a bound.

Every fall we surprise *Lepus americanus* in the act of changing his clothes. And every spring we see him change them back.

He's common around most of Vermont, and conspicuous twice a year as he adopts a new color combination.

Last autumn I took some friends for an afternoon drive to see Vermont's famed fall foliage. We saw several snowshoe hares—some in the summer pelage of brown, others in varying shades of gray as the fur ends whitened. In fact, it's this color change that gives rise to their other name: varying hare.

By the time winter came they would be white all over—all but the tips of their ears, dark eyes and twitching noses. More than once I've spotted a hare under a fir tree by the twinkle of that dark, irrepressible nose.

The name "snowshoe" fits just as well. Along with the whitening of the fur, the feet begin to grow a mass of stiff hairs. Then their owner can pad over the soft snow without sinking, while enemies flounder far behind.

Along with the tracks of this big hare in that first winter whiteness we look for those of another snowshoer. I don't see its tracks as often as I do those of the hare, but they're just as distinctive. They belong to the ruffed grouse.

In the fall this bird begins to sprout comblike fringes along its toes. By snowtime the foot area has been doubled. Then the "forest hen" can continue its unhurried walk, placing one foot directly in front of the other, right over the top of a snowdrift. It grows a set of feather leggings, too, for the winter months.

December finds us in our woods, picking out our Christmas tree. This year, two Saturdays before Christmas, the six of us started out. Jack frolicked before us, his plumed tail waving. Doglike, he visited the stumps and fenceposts, showing the same interest in them as do his city cousins in their fire hydrants.

We picked out a fine fir and took it back to the house. The next day a friend came looking for a spruce. As we took to the woods again, we saw another trail something like Jack's. This time, however, the animal had "tracked" perfectly, with the hind feet stepping exactly into the front footprints. The result was a long line of single tracks a foot apart, apparently made by a one-legged dog.

Like Jack, the creature had sniffed at every grass clump. Doglike, too, it had solemnly visited the fence posts, for it was that tireless little trotting wild dog, the red fox.

We stopped and inspected the tracks. Here it had pounced on a hummock in hopes of finding a mouse nest. There it had chewed a few dried grapes that still clung to the vine. Somehow I was reminded of a single mountain sheep we saw in a national park one summer—a sheep which looked with amusement, probably, at a score of humans creeping up on it with their cameras in hopes of getting a picture. Yet that sheep, or this fox, would hardly receive a moment's notice from these same humans if it were in a zoo. How much more valuable is a single wild fox or mountain sheep in its natural setting than a whole cageful of cooped-up, hand-fed animals! Wildlife refuges and parks may not bring in much revenue, but some things will not be measured in dollars.

I remember a visit to my grandfather's farm. There was a new fall of snow. I puzzled at some tracks I noticed running out from beneath the barn. "What makes a track with a line in the middle?" I asked at supper. "Something dragging something?"

Grandpa looked at the tracks the next morning. "Just a plain rat," he said. "And he was dragging my pocketbook."

It was years before I understood what he meant. Of course the line was made by the rat's tail in the snow, but Grandpa referred to the tremendous economic loss due to these European imports. One estimate says our food costs twice as much as it should because of rat loss.

Yet there is a plus side to their ledger. For *Rattus norvegicus* in his albino fur and pink eyes is the mainstay of much of our laboratory work. Without the white rat, biologists would know vastly less about disease control, nutrition, genetics. Rattus, in his scavenger's cloak, spread the horror of Plague; Rattus, in his laboratory smock, may soon help us defeat cancer.

"As the days get longer," the old-timers say, "the cold gets stronger." Even though the minutes of sunlight pile up after the short days of December, the snow begins to pile up too.

In many ways a heavy snowfall is better than a meager one in our Green Mountains. A hard-pressed grouse, just ahead of a horned owl, can plunge into its sheltering depths, sometimes even spending the night there. We once saw where a fox had pounced on a drift where a grouse had dived in. The grouse, though, had cannily tunneled to one side, so the fox had gone away empty.

Snow may be a help to the deer, too. They can stand on it and reach twigs that would otherwise be inaccessible to them. However, if it gets too thick it hampers their movements. Then they tend to "yard up" in certain areas, soon exhausting the available food supply.

Heavy snow also raises the rabbits up to where they can chew on the tips of bushes. We often note the peculiar slanting cuts made as they tip their heads for best use of those buck teeth.

Each spring as the thaws come, my meadows are laced with a surprising network. It's composed of mouse trails through the snow. Packed harder than the rest of the snow, they are slow to melt. In winter the trails are marked only by occasional holes where the trailmaker came to the surface. In summer they are overhung with grass. So most of the time I am not aware of them.

During a thaw, however, these interminable runways hint at the tremendous numbers of these little rodents, sometimes called the most successful mammal group of all time. There may be two hundred meadow mice alone on an acre—to say nothing of half a dozen other species.

Often I see their tracks on the snow. They leap or run if the surface is hard, emulate a little snowplow if it's soft.

Once I followed a mouse trail along our fence. It ended suddenly. To either side were a few parallel lines on the snow. A few feet further, I understood. A little tuft of gray fur lay on the snow. A hawk or owl, with perfect timing, had found its dinner. The parallel lines at the end of the trail were marks of its wing feathers as it flapped upward with its prey.

I saw some of the strangest prints in the snow one bright afternoon. They were tiny—scarcely four inches long—and little wider than a kitchen match. They could hardly be seen, except when the sun was low and the shadows slanted. Beginning and ending with a hole in the snow, they were apparently where some tiny creature had come up, crept along, and gone down again. "Decipher us, if you can," they challenged.

It took me a full year to solve the riddle. Finally, one February day, I got my evidence. The snow was covered with caterpillars—velvety-brown, slowly crawling along over its crumbly surface. As they crept, they made the delicate little trails.

Why do tropical people wear white? For the same reason that my insects wore brown. Light colors reflect the sun's rays; dark ones absorb them. As the sun gets higher in the sky, its rays filter down through the snow and stir the insects. Their dark-colored bodies become tiny self-enclosed heating pads as they make their way to the surface.

I've seen crane flies, spiders and beetles on the snow. In fact, a little insect called the springtail is so common around tree trunks or exposed rocks that it's dubbed the "snow flea."

A walk in the snow on our hundred acres is never the same. One time we find the sharp hoofprints of a deer as it sinks deep in a drift. Again we follow the lacy trail of a running deer mouse until it unaccountably ends at the bottom of a bush. Then, raising our eyes, we may find the little creature at home, comfortably warm in an abandoned bird's nest.

Every snow story, from the scales of a birch catkin scattered by a feeding grouse overhead to the rounded pug-marks of a wildcat, is a tale that's never been told before.

CHAPTER FOUR

Groundhog Day

"GROUNDHOG DAY—half your hay." That's what it says in my old Vermont almanac. What it means, of course, is that the winter is about half over on that second day of February. But no two years are ever the same.

For that matter, no two groundhogs are the same. Tradition has it that if *Marmota monax*—just call him a woodchuck if you prefer—sees his shadow on the fateful day, he'll scurry back for another six weeks' sleep. If there's no shadow to frighten him, he'll stay out—and spring is on its way. But

31

while Marmota in my north pasture fulfills his role, Marmota in my south pasture may be sound asleep.

Or vice versa. Like most of my wild neighbors, the ground-hog doesn't go by the books, or the calendar.

One late January day we saw the horses with what Peg calls their "watchful look." This consists of grazing, head downward, in apparent peace, but with ears pointed toward a strange object. If the children go over the pasture hill so they're no longer seen from the house, I know the direction they've taken by looking at the horses' ears. Now the horses were munching timothy hay spread out on the snow. Those ears, however, told us we were missing something.

We stood, watching quietly. "Do you suppose there's a deer in the woods?" Peg asked.

As if in answer, both horses raised their heads at once. But they didn't look off into the woods. Instead, they stared at a bundle of hay some fifteen feet from them. It was behaving and carrying on as no hay should. It gave a little jump, then began to crawl along the ground.

I snatched the binoculars. But they weren't necessary. At a snort from the horses, the hay gave a violent start. Then a familiar form rose above it. It was a woodchuck, a week ahead of his Day. Wakened, perhaps by the tread of hoofs, he had burst out through the hay into the bright sunlight. Now he sat up in accepted rodent fashion, casting a fine shadow with no concern at all.

He helped himself to the hay for ten minutes and then disappeared. "Do you suppose he just didn't get to bed in November—or couldn't he wait until February?" the children asked. It could have been either, for this huge ground squirrel often suffers from insomnia. I've seen him at least once every month of the year.

My hundred acres are full of fretful sleepers. One Washington's Birthday we took the children for a walk on the hill. A good February thaw was in the making. The snow had settled and we could hear the pasture brook as it rushed along beneath it. The sun was almost hot.

We stopped to rest on a patch of bare earth. A small red maple shared the patch with us. One of its limbs had broken in a wind, and the sweet sap oozed down the trunk.

Suddenly I heard an exclamation from Alison. "Butterflies, Dad? In *February?*"

We followed her gaze. There on the trunk, sipping the sap with their long uncoiled tube-mouths, were three Mourning Cloak butterflies. While thousands of their relatives slept, these restless little insects were out in the winter sunshine. They were trying out the new wings they had developed last fall.

We could see the blue-bordered wings with cream edging, the rich red-brown main colors which cause the British to call them Camberwell Beauty. I remembered the dark-bodied snow fleas I had seen at the base of another tree. Here, too, the dark color was storing a fraction of the sun's energy as heat.

"What brings them out while everything else is still asleep?" Alison wondered. But all I could do was shrug. Most other butterflies and moths stow away for months, or fling the torch to a new generation of eggs and caterpillars waiting in insulated jackets and fur coats. But this little aerialist doesn't know when to quit. Its winter sleep seems to be just a series of naps between thaws.

We watched until they had had their fill. Then the little squadron lifted from the trunk and took off across the snow fields for the nearby woods.

Later that evening we thought of our butterflies. The mercury had sunk with the sun, and winter was upon us once more. Somewhere, in some hollow tree or rocky crevice, slumbered the Camberwell Beauties, wings folded back-to-back above their bodies, legs tucked up securely. If some lucky mouse or shrew didn't find them, perhaps they'd fly three or four times more before the real spring arrived, bringing with it their myriads of late-rising relatives.

As the children discussed the fate of the butterflies I recalled one time I'd been worried about another light sleeper I'd found on my boyhood farm.

"Daddy, come quick! Oh, come quick!" I can still hear my own childish voice as I rushed, out of breath, up from the brook to the farmhouse.

My father must have learned what to expect—which was anything—from these urgent requests. He shrugged himself into his jacket and accompanied me outside.

"There's a turtle under the ice, and he's drowning!" I was almost in tears. "We've got to save him!"

My father jerked his axe from the chopping block and we went down to rescue the turtle. However, the poor creature had other ideas. He cocked a brown eye at us through two feet of water and six inches of ice. Then he did his version of the three-yard dash. One leg made its way out of the shell and pulled him forward a few inches. Soon it was aided by another. Slowly, slowly, he made his way to the opaque white ice at the edge of the brook.

We never rescued him. I lay awake long that night wondering at a cruel nature which would do such terrible things to helpless creatures.

Eventually I found out the truth. The wood turtle takes his sleep in small doses. Far from drowning, he lives at such a slow speed in winter that he requires little oxygen. I've seen one resting on the bottom of a beaver pond in the same place for two days. Yet he wasn't really asleep, for his head would be partly out when we arrived, and he'd regard us through half-closed lids.

"He looks like I feel after the alarm clock goes off," smiled Peg.

I've seen frogs grotesquely kicking along under the ice. Once I watched a blacksnake on a stone wall on a winter afternoon. It was so cold that it could barely flicker its tongue. Any sunny day will bring the flies out of the attic of our old farmhouse. They buzz against the windows to get out, while outside the chickadees beat against the glass in an effort to get at them.

Even that overcoated woodland clown, the black bear, is just drowsing. One of my neighbors, hunting snowshoe rabbits last winter, curiously poked a snow-covered mound at the base of an old hemlock. His skin began to crawl when the "mound" slowly raised its head and snuffed at him.

"Hibernation," says my dictionary, "is the passing of the winter in a lethargic or torpid condition." If Bruin falls short of being a true hibernator, one of our little back-yard neighbors does not. This we discovered one day when we moved the granary.

We wanted this little building taken off its foundation and put up on a hillside for a cabin. "Wait 'til the ground's hard," advised our mover. "Then I'll hitch a tractor to her, put her on a couple of skids, and she'll slide over the snow easy as shootin' fish in a barrel."

So we waited. Sure enough, she slid. And then we discovered a striped little hibernator. He'd been uncovered when the building was pulled aside.

In the summer there is no creature much quicker than the little Eastern chipmunk, but in winter there's none slower. Coiled up in a half-bushel of maple seeds he'd gathered, this

little fellow's fires were banked astonishingly low. We thought
at first they were out completely. He was nearly as cold as a
clod of earth.

I picked him up and tried to detect breathing or heartbeat.
No success. A patch of skin had been torn away, but the
wound didn't bleed. We tossed him back and forth like a base-
ball, but he never stirred.

"Now where can we put him, Dad?"

I thought for a moment. "Well, we can't leave him here.
He'll freeze without any shelter."

Finally we put him in a bushel basket with his seeds, and
deposited him down cellar. By afternoon his little flanks were
moving. Next morning he was gone.

Later I learned more about creatures in hibernation. Although the pulse may slow to a twentieth of its rate and the
animal may breathe only once in five minutes, its sense of touch
is still keen. If we hadn't been so rough with him, he might
have snoozed the winter out in his basket. As it was, the un-
dignified treatment had been too much for him. He took off
for parts where there wasn't so much company.

A friend of mine at Middlebury College spends part of his
winter vacation investigating bats in caves. Like the chipmunk
they are slowed down almost to a complete stop.

But if winter puts some of my animal neighbors to sleep, it
goads others to frenzied activity. In the fall the white-footed
mice sometimes move into our walls from the fields outside.
They are peaceful creatures, with snow-white underparts, large
ears and appealing eyes. However, their stay is often cut short
by the appearance of a terror no larger than they are. I hear
him in the night, talking to himself in a strange buzzing
squeak as he dashes about. Suddenly there is a wild commo-
tion in the walls and the buzzing stops. Then I know that the

shrew—for that is what it is—has claimed one of the mice.

One winter a friend brought me a shrew. I put on a pair of leather gloves and cupped it in my hands. At once I could feel an intense vibration. It reminded me of the hum of an electric clock. I have seldom felt closer to the very heart of life itself. The hum was the combination of the shrew's fantastic body activities—his breathing at more than 100 gasps per minute, and his heartbeat at something around 1000.

Winter must be a trial for this little warrior. His digestive canal is so short that he sometimes eats twice his own weight every twenty-four hours to survive. Shrews captured in the evening have been known to starve overnight.

Everything that moves is potential food—even another shrew. As one scientist observed to me, "There's no such thing as two shrews. They can't stand each other. Put two in a cage together and you'll have just one left in five minutes."

I've always wondered how such antisocial little mites could abide each other long enough to beget young. Apparently they do, though, because next to the rodents they're probably the most common mammal on my hundred acres.

Even some plants can't seem to wait for the alarm clock. One Saturday morning Roger and Alison went for a walk. When they came back they smelled so much that Peg would hardly let them in the house.

"Whoof! Where on earth have you *been?*"

"Nowhere, Mother; just down by the brook, that's all."

"And how did you happen to run into a skunk?"

"Why, we didn't see any skunks, Mom," said Roger. His eyes twinkled, and Alison stifled a giggle. "We just brought you back these."

He reached a muddy mitten into his coat pocket. One by one he pulled out four red-and-green-striped cups. They looked like loosely rolled thick leaves. Inside of each could be seen an upright light-colored object, like an inch-long ear of corn.

"Skunk cabbages," said Roger innocently. "Your first spring bouquet, Mom."

Sometimes I wish his eyes weren't so sharp. The flower of *Symplocarpus foetidus*—whose name matches its odor—barely pokes above the mud of a March brookside. Early spring flies, attracted by the smell, wander over its upright yellow spadix, spreading the pollen. And we, somewhat less attracted, hung Roger's coat out on the back porch for several days.

I used to think that if you couldn't find pussy willows or crocuses, there just weren't any spring flowers to be had. Now I know otherwise. Get in your car or take a walk to a spot where the sun shines on a south-sloping hillside. There you're likely to find a number of flowers ahead of their time. Where a massive rock or old stump has soaked up the sun's heat, you may find plants already green, warming themselves against this natural stove.

I once picked a little cluster of Spring Beauties in March, though they don't appear elsewhere until April. When I got them home, I discovered a tiny green caterpillar on one of the leaves. Like the plants, woodchucks, and even the chipmunks and bats, it had just been biding its time.

SPRING

CHAPTER FIVE

Ice Out!

WHEN THE ICE goes out of a river or brook, it's a real event to those along its shores. So it is with our little river in Lincoln.

All winter the stream has been still. At least that's the way it appears. Under the white mantle which cloaks it, the roar of the water is reduced to a gurgle. Foxes, mice, shrews and weasels which formerly found it a barrier now use it as a highway. We never tire of standing at our bridge and trying to decipher the maze of tracks which accumulate after every snow.

Spring break-up is a thing I'll never get used to. Although

the pattern is about the same, the results are always startling. The sun is warm and persistent for three or four days. It melts the snow fastest in the vicinity of hummocks, bushes, trees and rocks. Finally each of these stands in a widening brown island in the snow.

Melt-water flows beneath the snow, decaying it from below while the sun strikes from above. Every little bank and path-edge comes alive with tiny trickles. These join with others to form little rivulets. On goes the water, ever joining, ever going faster.

Finally it empties into the river. From a thousand temporary little brooks it empties. Each cupful swells the volume of the larger stream.

Hourly the snow on the river turns to slush. A faint ripple is noticeable on its surface. But still the river-ice holds, though it now is several inches below the top of the awakening stream.

The sun goes down behind West Mountain, but the evening stays warm. Peg and I go out on the bridge and look at the river. Will this be the night?

All during supper we eat in silence. Roger goes out to the back porch. "Forty-five degrees, Dad. Think the ice will break before I go to bed?"

"I don't know, Roger. I've given up trying to predict it."

"Well, when it goes out will you wake me up?"

There's a rumbling sound. Tom rushes to the window. "Darn it! Just a lumber truck coming down the road!"

We wait. Janice does her German. Alison and Roger play a game of dominoes. I help Tom with his Latin. Peg does the dishes as quietly as she can. Every few minutes someone goes to the front door.

"Nothing yet. I hope it doesn't happen after we're all asleep."

It usually does. Or at any rate it happens just when we're

least prepared. Perhaps the phone rings; or Janice goes in to play the piano; or we think we're hearing another truck on the gravel road. But one moment it's winter. And five seconds later it is spring.

The ice doesn't begin to go out. It doesn't start to go out. It just goes—all at once, in a monstrous rush. One second the river will be calm clear water over the green ice, with patches of snow stubbornly holding out against the slowly rising water. Then there's a crack somewhere, a rumble, a roar—and in scarcely more time than it takes to read this sentence, the whole river is in a fury.

Great chunks of ice careen along like chips. Some of them outweigh an automobile. The water turns black and terrible. It rises minute by minute. Dead logs, ice, even boulders rumble along, scouring the rocks and bushes at the river's edge.

Our house, only fifty feet away from the riverbank, shakes as in an earthquake. Dishes rattle, windows set up a vibration until we have to wedge them tight with chunks of cardboard. Jack growls uneasily.

We dash into our coats and rush out to the bridge.

We seldom say much as we watch the ice go out. There is little that can be put into words. No ocean traveler, standing on the fantail of a liner, sees a greater display of boiling, tumbling water. Our New Haven River won't average forty feet wide in normal times through the whole town of Lincoln; yet "ice out" is such a spectacle that everybody rushes to its shores to watch.

"I've seen a thousand spring thaws," twinkled one old-timer. "And I ain't tired of 'em yet. I'll still get out of bed to see the danged ice leave town."

Sometimes, like the woodchuck or the Mourning Cloak, the river gets optimistic too soon. The ice may go out in January, but soon it builds back up. Its final retreat, however, is unmistakable.

Next day the river is clean, scoured, free flowing. Along both sides are mighty chunks, washed there on the crest and deserted by the ebbing water. Bushes and trees are scrubbed clean of bark on the upriver side. Boulders in midstream may wear flat caps of green-white ice, sometimes tilted at a crazy angle. Where the ice jammed momentarily so as to force the river through a new channel, there may be ice floes out in the middle of a meadow. Sometimes they are three hundred feet from the now-chastened water.

I may have one of the biggest farms in the United States. My deed says that the property goes to a certain post in the northeast corner. Two years ago the river switched its channel. It ran away with my post and several dozen feet of wire. I like to think the post floated all the way to Lake Champlain, north to the St. Lawrence River, and out into the Atlantic Ocean. Actually, it's probably snagged fifty feet downstream.

Once we took a trip to the west coast. All along the way were numerous souvenir shops. Many of them had a jar in which stones were tumbled by electric motor until they were worn smooth and shiny by pumice or other grit before being mounted as costume jewelry.

Up and down our river are large and small potholes, made by the same action. Sand grains, lodging in cracks in a rock, swirl around and enlarge their hole. Pebbles follow, rounding it out some more. Finally sizable boulders may tumble in and grind away with every spring flood.

One pothole near my house is large enough to hold a horse. But this is small compared to one a geologist told me about. It was so wide and deep that when a mastodon stumbled into it, he couldn't get out. Centuries later men dug his bones out of their circular grave. Such a hole indicates the thunderous power of water at flood stage.

Powerful though our river is at its crest, it's a peaceful ripple compared to the mighty force exerted by a far greater river which once overflowed the northern section of our country. This was the river of ice which geologists have identified as the last great glacier. Its awesome strength was attested to me one day as I stood with a friend on top of Mt. Abraham, Vermont's fifth-highest peak.

"I'd certainly like to have *this* rock in my rock garden," she said as she looked at a massive boulder of white quartz balanced on a ledge a few feet from the summit.

"Go ahead. Take it home with you. I'm sure nobody would mind."

"And how do you suggest I get it there?"

A derrick would be needed to lift it and a flatcar to haul it. It was as big as an automobile, yet it had been deposited four thousand feet in the air by that icy river of long ago.

Perhaps it was transported from a ledge just a few miles away. Perhaps it came hundreds of miles from northern Canada. It's hard to say. The ice sheet which covered our northern states was like a bulldozer as it moved south, picking material up here and depositing it there.

In college I learned that it got as far as the Connecticut coastline. There it finally halted. Then, slowly, it began to melt back. As it did, it abandoned the mass of debris it had been pushing.

That mass is still there. Today it's known as Long Island.

The scenery was changed enormously by the relentless force and weight of the ice sheet. Mountains were scalped. River valleys were scoured deep and wide as probing tentacles of ice sagged into them. The Finger Lakes of New York State are evidence of such a scouring. They show well the direction of travel of the great scoop—from north to south.

Not only are its aftereffects seen, but they may be felt as well. On April 10, 1962, our peaceful Green Mountain State was shaken by one tremor after another as an earthquake jostled its northern section. School children were herded out into the streets; residents fled their homes thinking their oil burners had exploded. Half a dozen shocks reverberated through the earth in the space of half an hour.

"It's difficult to pinpoint the exact cause of a New England earthquake," a geologist told me. "Possibly it was internal stresses in the mountains. But that old ice sheet was tremendously heavy as it lay on the land. In some places it compressed the earth several hundred feet. There's evidence that the ground is still springing back up. Today's tremor was perhaps a little of that recoil."

If this was indeed the case, it brings a whole new dimension to those glacial ages. For not only did the great ice sheet scrape down to bedrock here and dump thousands of boulders there, but its ponderous advance must have made the very earth's crust sink.

Even as the land groaned and life fled before its advance, the great mass was at the same time preparing the stage for another movement of earth. This one, to come so many years later, would be man-made. It's the reshuffling of thousands of tons of sand and gravel for construction of roads, concrete bridges and skyscrapers. One symbol of this is a small wooden sign posted on the outskirts of town.

"Gravl. By the Yd. or by the JoB," the sign says. Its owner had dug into a rounded hillside behind his house. There you could buy one cubic yard of pebbles and sand, or a thousand.

Little does he realize, I suspect, that his rounded hill is a "kame," or mound of debris left by the glacier. Often these kames contain perfectly sorted sand and pebbles in distinct layers, deposited by melting water from the great sheet of ice. These low tear-drop hills, sometimes elongated from north to south like huge compass-needles in Braille, are common to the New England scene. My "Gravl"-pit owner is probably unaware, too, that his little power loader is in partnership with forces unleashed some ten thousand years ago.

But sometimes the glacier scattered its rocks wholesale. Its method was rather like that of a man who makes a bathing beach on a lake shore in dead of winter. All he need do is wheel loads of sand out onto the ice. In the spring, when the ice melts, down goes the sand to the bottom.

The same thing has happened, on a gigantic scale, to our New England landscape. As the glacier melted, its burden of rocks and gravel was lowered gently to earth. Wherever a rock happened to "touch bottom," there it would stay—even if "bottom" happened to be a mountaintop. This is what happened on Mt. Abraham, and 6,288-foot Mt. Washington, which thereby received a jumble of boulders.

These round rocks are found in impossible places all over our Northeast—hundred-ton "balancing rocks" on a ledge, or boulders so huge that early road builders ran their highways around them.

Many of our New England towns have their "frog rock"— a bit of glacial debris painted with eyes and mouth. On the Long Trail in Lincoln are two massive granite chunks. They are all by themselves in the woodland. Each is half the size of a house. They lie on top of the ground, and the trail goes between them. It's this certainty of the unexpected that adds so much to the charm of New England.

Today my little stream nibbles away at the rocky rubble

left by the glacier. In many places it runs over bedrock, exposed and scratched in long parallel lines by the icy invader. Those north-and-south scratches are still visible on many ledges and rock outcrops of New England. Look for them the next time you're hiking or picnicking.

"It says here that when the Pilgrims came to this country, they landed on a rock," Roger said one evening.

"Huh!" exploded Tom, fresh from helping me take stones out of our garden. "Where else could they have landed?"

CHAPTER SIX

Bluebirds

LAST YEAR the first bluebird came on the fourth of April. The year before that he arrived on the ninth. This year he arrived on the third.

He looks over my birdhouses and picks out the one he likes. Then, morning after morning he sits on it, uttering his liquid "chur-a-wee" while our hearts grow glad.

For two years no little lady has come to share his nest. Finally, after several hopeful days, his song is heard no more. Then we know that this little cousin of the robin and nightingale has moved on.

Soon he'll enchant some other dooryard with his song. Some other family will exclaim over the astonishing blue of his back, the rich salmon of his breast. But here, too, he'll probably sing alone.

Whole generations of Americans have marked the coming of spring by the appearance of the bluebirds. Now it seems the birds' days are numbered. They are in deep trouble.

Winsome Bluebird, as Thornton Burgess called him, is partially in danger from the very creatures who love him. When the farm orchard included a few old apple trees, there were plenty of hollow stubs to serve as nesting sites. The old trees were an insect paradise, and the bluebirds found enough food for their young.

Today, however, the old apple tree is cut down. Likewise, the hollow fencepost, once a fine bluebird site, is replaced by a metal one, or by electric fencing. So the bluebird is faced with a housing shortage.

There's another reason for its plight which first came to my attention several springs ago. Out beyond the barn is a birdhouse on a post. I had seen a bluebird around it several days, but finally it disappeared. When I went to clean out the birdhouse much later, I understood. It contained the nest of an English sparrow. Underneath this was a perfect nest of a bluebird, containing four blue-green eggs. The little songster had been nesting there until the sparrow took over. Small wonder that the blatant, black-and-brown European import has been called the "feathered rat"!

Starlings, too, will nest in a treehole, no matter what other bird claims it. I've watched them wait for woodpeckers or flickers to finish hollowing out a tree stub. Then, when the hard-working carpenters are finished, the starlings drive them away. The bluebirds, of course, are no match for such robbers.

BLUEBIRDS

Some five years ago I sat with a friend in his back yard.

"Look at those darned starlings!" he cried. "They're going to take over every birdhouse in the place!"

We watched as a starling peered into the entrance hole of a bluebird house. It was completely unimpressed with the dives and chirps of the frantic owners. It went into the box for a moment, then flew away. In two minutes it was back with a wisp of straw.

"How in thunder am I going to keep him from nesting there —short of shooting him?" sputtered my friend.

His wife spoke up. "Dick, he looks as if he's quite a bit bigger than the bluebirds. How about making the hole smaller?"

We got a stepladder and tacked a piece of tin so that it slightly covered one side of the hole. Then we settled back to wait.

The bluebirds had their doubts about the new object. But the starling did not. He flew straight to the box, a big chunk of grass in his yellow bill. The bluebirds forgot their suspicions and dived at him again.

Full of self-confidence, he poked his head into the box. But his shoulders wouldn't fit. Back out again, he tried it once more. Then he hopped up on top of the birdhouse and looked down accusingly.

After he had the hole thoroughly cowed, he tried it again. Still it wouldn't work. So once again he sat on top and glared at it. Finally he flew off in disgust, still clutching his grass. The triumphant bluebirds chased him all the way to the street.

Since then my friend has been more careful in measuring his bird boxes. A hole $1\frac{1}{2}$ inches wide is perfect for bluebirds but too small for starlings. If the box is placed away from buildings, English sparrows show less interest in it.

Competition, however, is not the last of the bluebird's woes. Chilly winter weather in the South has cost the lives of many birds. Those that have survived to come north may be threatened by our current pesticide programs. "Poisoning of bluebirds by insecticides has so far not been scientifically proved," says Robert Gannon in *Reader's Digest* for March 1962. "But bluebirds feed largely on insects, and many ornithologists point out that if poisoned insects are eaten, toxin is passed on to the birds, and if they don't die, their eggs may be infertile."

Right-size nesting boxes and care with chemicals are just a couple of the tricks that benefit wildlife. I'll never forget a question put to our college class as we took an outdoor examination in conservation.

We stood next to a fencerow which had grown up along an old wall. Cherry, serviceberry, dogwood, raspberry and nut trees made up the vegetation.

"Why do you suppose these particular species are growing here?" the professor asked.

We shuffled our feet. "Because they do well next to walls?" one student suggested.

"Is it because they're hardy and fast growing?" asked another.

"Perhaps it's because the whole field was like this before the farmer cleared it," ventured another.

None of us guessed the answer, simple as it was. The trees and bushes were there largely because the birds and animals had placed them there. Squirrels had hidden nuts and acorns in the wall. Birds had flown there and left the unharmed seeds of cherries and serviceberries in their droppings. Mice had scampered along with raspberries and apple seeds.

"If you want to know what the wildlife of an area would prefer," said our teacher, "look at the fencerows. And," he continued, "if you want to know what to plant for them, look at those same rows."

Since then I've often seen his statement borne out. I've watched gray squirrels run along a stone wall with apples in their mouths. Fox droppings are loaded with blackberry seeds in season. They, too, use the ground along the old fence as a highway.

The chipmunk is common along fences, where it often hoards its seeds. I recall my hibernating 'munk asleep on his mattress of maple seeds. If a single seed had escaped his hunger, there beneath the ground, a potential tree would be in the making.

"The deep forest and the open fields," our professor told us, "usually have very specialized animal life. If you want to see most of your common birds and animals, go to the forest openings—the wood roads, and places where trees have been cut. Brush piles are good spots, too. Or go to the forest edge. There you get bushes, shrubs, young growth of all kinds. An overgrown fencerow extends that 'edge' out into the field. Sometimes it connects wildlife areas by a valuable highway."

Even my little bluebird neighbor stands to benefit from this "edge effect." More shrubbery means more insects, berries and nesting sites for a hundred species of birds and animals. But sometimes a habitat can be too favorable.

"How in the dickens am I going to plant a garden if the deer eat all my crops?" asked an irate neighbor.

"Feed 'em a good crop of lead," another answered. "They'll get full awful quick."

Before I came to Vermont I might have shuddered at such a cold-blooded viewpoint toward this graceful soft-eyed animal.

But now I can sympathize—both with the deer and the farmer. Hundreds of abandoned farms all over our state have grown up to brambles and bushes, and the deer have increased apace. With the mountain lion, wolf and lynx gone, there is little to stop them. Estimates place five deer on every square mile of our Green Mountain National Forest, or one animal for every three persons in the entire state.

It's a big problem. Not only for the deer, which excites the imagination of most anyone, but for the bluebird at the other end of the cycle of abundance. Over the rest of the country are such vanishing Americans as the wolverine, the American crocodile, timber wolf, grizzly bear, trumpeter swan, whooping crane and others.

"It's as if we were standing astride a seesaw," my professor concluded that day. "We can knock the whole thing out of kilter by throwing our weight around the wrong way. The 'balance of nature' is not just a figure of speech. It's amazingly delicate—worked out only after eons of trial and error on the part of living things.

"We've eliminated the heath hen and the passenger pigeon," he said. "We tried to do the same thing to the bison, the sea otter and the fur seal. I don't know what will be next."

I just hope it's not the bluebird. Spring will never be the same without him.

CHAPTER SEVEN

Mess o' Greens

SEVERAL TIMES each spring
the whole family goes looking for what my father used to call
"a mess o' greens." Sometimes we take a kettle or basket and
sit on the lawn, carefully cutting dandelions at the soil line.
Other times we search for curly dock, or pokeweed sprouts,
or the downy-white shoots of milkweed. But the finest greens,
to our way of thinking, come from the marsh marigold, or
"cowslip."

It grows with wet feet, does this yellow-flowered relative
of the buttercup. Each April it pokes up along brooks and

swamps from Newfoundland to Saskatchewan, from South Carolina to Nebraska. Its smooth heart-shaped leaves and green buds are crisp as lettuce.

We put on boots or rubbers and fill a couple of pails, to the accompaniment of a chorus of spring frogs, with red-winged blackbirds overhead. The journey to get the plant, the picking on a joyous spring day, and later the enjoyment of the steaming greens with butter trickling through them—these are the wonderful, homely extras that come with a life in the country.

"It's a lot easier just to buy a package of spinach at the store," suggested Alison hopefully as she helped Peg and Janice pick over the latest mess o' greens from the swamp.

"Yes, but it's not half so much fun," said Janice.

Alison, however, wouldn't give up. "But you get green stamps at the store."

Our friends Dick and Freda Koenig also get their greens without benefit of stamps.

"What gets me," said Freda one day, "is the way that tons of food go begging in our woods and fields every season."

We were dining on boiled nettles at the moment. "Not one person in fifty seems to know that young nettles are as good 'greens' as you can get," said Dick.

I could vouch for his statement. Those little nettle sprouts were delicious. Their famous stingers had wilted harmlessly with the first touch of hot water.

"Over in Germany where I grew up," Dick continued, "we learned to pick all kinds of plants and roots when we were little children. Here, in America, most people just don't seem to bother. They'll drive past a whole field of narrow-leaved dock to look for greens in a supermarket. And yet that same dock is sold at a fancy price in many stores."

I recalled my own experience along these lines. One April

noon I wandered along the streets of New York City. I surveyed the restaurant menus pasted in the windows. "Fiddle-head salad—$1.00," said one. "Watercress sandwich—$.50," said another. "Turkey with wild rice—$2.00," said still another. There were also menus on which you could have dandelion greens, "Country cowslips," chickory and "wild asparagus."

All of these, except the turkey and wild rice, can be had right on my hundred acres. The wild rice grows in waving profusion along the shores of a marsh a few miles away. Turkey, too, is a creature of the wild, now domesticated.

Fiddleheads, the delight of the gourmet, are nothing more than the croziers, or sprouts, of new ferns whose tightly coiled tips look like the scroll of a violin. They appear at the edge of meadows and along roadsides as spring advances. Several kinds can be used, but the ostrich-fern, *Pteretis pennsylvanica,* is the one that usually makes its way to the best restaurants. Its relative, *Pteridium aquilinum,* known to my country neighbors as "bracken" or "brakes," comes out of the chef's kitchen as wild asparagus. Makings for watercress salad and watercress sandwiches grow in the clear cold of my pasture brook. All you need to supply is the bread and salad dressing. Chicory is angrily uprooted by farmers, who dislike the coarse blue-flowered weed in their hay crop, but its young shoots are proudly borne to the epicure's table as "French endive" and its dried roots become "chicory tea."

Even domestic weeds come in for their share of honors.

"Looks like the weeds in your garden are as bad as those in mine," grinned a visitor last summer.

Later we sat down to dinner. He enthused over the meal—especially the Green Mountain Spinach. "Where on earth do you get Green Mountain Spinach?" he asked.

Peg smiled. "That's a name we made up. Most people call it lamb's-quarters, goosefoot, or even pigweed. It was the smooth pale green weed you saw between the rows in our garden. We think it's delicious, and put some up in our freezer every year."

When he went home that evening our guest took a paper bag full of "weeds" to his wife.

If he had come a few weeks later we could have fed him another of our unplanted garden crops. I recall the struggle I used to have with it as a child.

"Purslane," said my father, hooking the sprawling plant with his hoe, "is the darnedest stuff. Turn it upside down in the hot sun, and it turns right over again. Next day it's growing as good as ever."

This may have been a slight exaggeration, but I cringe every time I think of how hard I tried to do away with the delicious stuff, sometimes called wild Portulaca, or pursley. It would have been so easy to put it in a pot, cook it like spinach, and serve with butter and salt if we'd only known. But I didn't learn how good it was until many years—and backaches—later.

Sometimes we pick the blossoms of the elderberries that hang over our spring. Then we dip them in batter and drop them in deep fat. They make wonderful fritters. A friend of ours does the same thing with dandelion heads.

I have been pleased to note that dandelions and chives have at last made high society: seed companies, nowadays, put these seeds in packets to sell.

A treat for our forebears who used to live off the land was the boiled root of that woodland oddity, the jack-in-the-pulpit. Cooked in several changes of water, it's known as "Indian turnip" and is delicious. Bears apparently love it, according to old-timers, and will dig it up in the spring for a tonic. But for human beings the raw material is bitterly acrid and leaves a painful aftertaste for an hour.

One time, years ago, this peppery root figured in a duel between my younger brother and myself. He was always tagging after us, so we determined to get rid of him.

"Can't I join your club?" he asked.

Don Brown and I shrugged. "I suppose so. But you've got to pass the Test."

"Sure," said Jimmy. "What do you want me to do?"

"Well—" my mind raced as I spoke, "you've got to bring us a jack-in-the-pulpit plant, roots and all."

We figured that would hold the kid brother for half an hour at least. But he was back in five minutes.

"Now," said I with a wink at Don, "here's the Test. You've got to eat a piece of the root."

Obligingly, trustingly, my little brother bit into it. The next instant he flung it from him and ran, tears streaming, for the house.

(Manfully, Jimmy didn't tell Mother what the trouble was. But he got even with us just the same. There was an abandoned car in which we used to play. It had a nest of wasps under the dashboard. Jimmy knew it and we didn't. One day as we were "driving," he gave it a tremendous whack with a stick. We sat there, trying to figure out why he was running. Then a white-hot jab in my bare leg made everything clear. The things kids do to keep themselves amused!)

In college we had to make a plant collection for botany class. I pressed a few little sorrel plants in bloom. When I looked at the blossoms later under a magnifier, a wave of memory swept over me. Going to the herbarium collection, I pulled out an envelope containing the flowers and pressed leaves of rhubarb. Sure enough, there were my little sorrel flowers—only expanded several times as I'd often seen them growing on the big garden plant.

I recalled picking sorrel with my grandmother for what she called a "pilgrim pie." I was struck at the time by how much it tasted like rhubarb. Now I knew the reason. Sorrel, with its little acid-filled leaves and three-cornered seeds, is a miniature relative of the huge-leaved, sour, pink-stemmed "pie plant."

Elms and mulberries, I learned, are same-family members. Apples, cherries and raspberries all belong to the rose family. Potato and eggplant are nightshades, and so on.

It hardly occurred to me that such family ties would be of more than academic interest until one day when I visited George Patterson's truck garden.

"Why do you have a couple of rows of radishes all around your cabbage field?" I asked.

"Keeps the cabbage bugs busy," he told me. He pulled up a radish. Its red globe was knotted and mined from the attacks of some kind of insect.

"Root maggots," he said. "With a huge cabbage field such as this, a lot of insects are attracted. But I learned somehow that they preferred radishes to cabbage—if they could get them. So I plant the radishes, and they siphon off the main attack of the maggots. Otherwise, the maggots would ruin my crop. Then, later, I destroy the radishes, and the insects, too."

A botanist wouldn't have been a bit surprised by this brand of biological warfare. Radish, cabbage, cauliflower, broccoli, turnip, all are crucifers—members of the *Cruciferae,* or mustard, family. In some areas, George told me, fields of wild mustard save turnips and brussels sprouts from cabbage worms.

Thus wild roses may serve as buffers against attacks by apple aphids, and your garden asters may suffer less from insects because the ragweed suffers more.

Don't the wild species serve as a nucleus for insects which attack cultivated plants? Undoubtedly they do. But in all of man's history, he has not succeeded in causing the demise of a single insect species. The little creatures are just too tough, too easily overlooked, to go the way of the Dodo. Besides, they are so tremendously motile as flying creatures that man can never get them under his figurative thumb. A farm free of every insect-loaded weed would still be vulnerable from other farms and the sky above.

George Patterson plants his radishes and harvests cabbages. I plant mine and harvest purslane. Maybe someday we'll meet at the grocery store and go shares on two bunches of radishes for a quarter.

We'll get green stamps, too.

CHAPTER EIGHT

Voices in the Dark

M Y SPINE was creeping.

On this April night I had taken my flashlight to look for frogs and their eggs in the big swamp near our house. The marsh had been ringing with sound when I arrived—the high note of the tiny spring peeper, the guttural croak of the wood frog, the splash of cold, unseen bodies in the water. Then, as I sneaked quietly in hopes of seeing the songsters, a floundering misstep had given me away.

A wave of shocked silence spread over the swamp. It was as I recovered my footing that my flashlight found the eyes.

65

They glittered at me steadily some twenty feet away. About five inches apart, they shone white and unflinching.

Bobcat, fisher-cat, raccoon, deer, fox, bear, lynx, panther— all these possibilities and impossibilities flashed through my mind. Not a frog was to be heard. The whole swamp seemed to wait as the Thing and I stared at each other along the flashlight beam.

Finally, from somewhere a few rods away, came the querulous note of a single frog. It was answered by another, and another. Still we stared as the notes became bolder.

Then the sound of frogs was all around us. They were oblivious to the battle of wits taking place across a stretch of black swamp water. I resolved that I'd let the Creature make the first move.

It did. But the move was completely unexpected. It was the very last thing that such an apparition should ever do.

It winked.

First it winked one eye, then the other. Then both of them blinked together. Then, as I stood aghast, it began to get cross-eyed. Those eyes started to turn in towards each other, still winking.

Just as I was beginning to doubt my sanity, the mystery resolved itself. With a flood of relief, I laughed out loud.

"Frogs!" I said to myself. "Nothing but frogs!"

Of course, that was it. The winking eyes were the throat pouches of two tiny spring peepers, distended to the size of a glistening marble as a sounding-board for their song. With each peep, the pouch would swell and seem to blink in the light of the flashlight. The whole thing had gone cross-eyed when one male, overcome by his own love-song, had sidled up to the other.

Slowly I waded closer to their hummock. The noise of the

swamp was deafening, with these two lusty peepers loudest of all. They paid no attention to the light, but clung wetly to the grass, singing their single note at the rate of once a second. Pitched nearly as high as a human can whistle, it seemed impossible that such volume could come from a little brown frog scarcely an inch long.

Later I captured a pair of spring peepers and took them home in a bottle. Together the two of them weighed a little more than one tenth of an ounce on my laboratory scales. Knowing that peepers can be heard a half-mile on a good night, we calculated how far the human voice could carry if we could shout proportionately. Our figure: some 10,000 miles, or halfway around the earth.

The voices of our peepers are perhaps the most characteristic sounds of a spring night. However, they are by no means the only ones. Nor are they the loudest. The shriek of a tree frog —a loud p-r-r-r-r-t! like some astounding night bird—can be deafening. Two settled in the trees just above our campfire one May night and made conversation almost impossible as they shouted across at each other. Finally I had to toss sticks up into the darkness to quiet them.

The bellow of the "Jug-o-rum," or bullfrog, from the lily pads sounds nearly as menacing as that of his bovine namesake. "Bloody-nouns," the settlers sometimes termed him in reference to the bass-fiddle sound of his call.

Toads and frogs of a dozen kinds make my swamp alive with their calls on a warm night. They almost drown out another great group of noisemakers which has shared the earth with the amphibians for the past 300 million years—the insects.

One night we were standing on our bridge, enjoying the sound of the river and listening to a single peeper which had chosen this swift water instead of a tranquil swamp. Suddenly Peg began to rub her arms and stamp her feet. At the same instant I heard around my ears and face tiny, incredibly high whines of sound. A little needle caught me on the neck; two others stabbed at my hairline.

"No-see-ums," I grimaced. "Guess we'd better go inside."

We fled the bridge, but not before half a dozen of these creatures had scored bull's-eyes. One of the smallest flies known in the United States, a single no-see-um could sit easily on the period at the end of this sentence. Yet their bite is so fierce that bears and deer will flee into the water to escape their torment. Luckily our section of New England suffers but little from them, and they're more a cause for amusement than alarm. They love to crawl into sheltered places—under wrist-watch bands, beneath collars, into eyebrows and even eye-lashes. Their almost inaudible piping is a part of existence on my hundred acres, and I've come to look forward to my an-nual summer bout with the "punkies" as a bit of the peppery spice of life in the country.

Many other insect sounds fill our spring night. A May beetle, or "June bug," goes rattling through the dark, whacking into a tree trunk and falling to earth with a thud. There's a scratch-ing in the leaves as he struggles upside down like a little turtle. Then there's a low buzz as he flies away again.

Sometimes I catch the red glare of his eyes in my flashlight beam, and he looks like an erratic spark from some unseen campfire. However, I don't keep the light on him too long, for he soon turns toward it, zeroed-in at full speed. I flick it off and duck quickly as he goes hurtling by. Like those of many another night-flier, the muscles on the side of his body exposed to the light are thereby weakened. Those on the dark side propel him more strongly and make him bank toward the light. Thus he is forced to fly into it whether he wishes to or not.

A leaf buzzes oddly as a moth miscalculates and flutters against it. All around us are rustlings and scrapings. One turns out to be from a caterpillar hunter, his fiery red-and-green beetle's body running over the ground. Another is made by a pair of sexton beetles, digging beneath a dead mouse to bury it as food for their larvae. Still another, sounding like the faint falling of rain, turns out to be the droppings from a horde of caterpillars. They are feeding overhead in the tree even as the caterpillar hunter races up the trunk, hot on their trail.

One night when we were camping out, Tom pulled at my sleeping bag in the dark. "What's that, Dad?"

We listened. There was a faint rustling, followed by a definite tattoo. It sounded like a little snare drum in the leaves. Again the rustling; again the tattoo. It went all around the outside of the tent.

At first I thought of mice, for they often drum on the ground with their forefeet—as, indeed, do skunks, rabbits, deer and many others. But, somehow, it didn't sound mammalian. It was too precise and mechanical, almost like a little toy that had been wound up and turned loose.

We got up, tiptoed outside, and listened some more. We pinpointed the sound just as a gray body ran out into a patch of moonlight. It stopped and was quiet for a moment. Then came the tattoo, like tiny hammers beating on a leaf.

I turned on the flashlight. In its beam stood the drummer— all eight fuzzy legs of him. It was a large male wolf spider, big enough to cover a teacup. He was engaged in one of the most hazardous occupations of his life. For he was advertising

69

his presence to any ladies of his kind—and woe to him if they happened to be hungry. To a spider anything may be prey, even if it is another spider.

We watched him for ten minutes in the early morning moonlight. He'd run for about half a yard, then stop. The two bulbous palps beside his fangs would rattle their message on a leaf or twig. He'd pause, waiting, then run on again. Five seconds for the run, three seconds to drum, eight or ten to wait—over and over, regular as a little metronome.

On he went into the woods, bearing his little mechanical wolf-whistle with him. Just as we were getting back to sleep, I heard the mournful whinny of a screech owl. I shuddered for the spider. He faced not only an uncertain reception from his own kind, but a more certain one from one of the best insect-, mouse- and spider-traps in my entire hundred acres.

Other voices in the night have accompanied me through our woods and meadows after dark. I've often heard the deep, wonderfully resonant hoot of a great horned owl that's hard to locate closer than a quarter of a mile somewhere out there in the dark. Twice I've heard him scream—a curdling sound like some maniacal tomcat, only deeper and more terrifying.

Once when Jack was a puppy, we heard a fox imitating him perfectly as he yipped and complained at being tied out for the night.

Sometimes the spring voices include the cackle of a V of geese, threading overhead on their way north. Peg once spotted them against the full moon. Like many birds they may migrate at night and feed during the day. That peerless soloist, the hermit thrush, whose wild song brings a lump to my throat, sometimes sings for an hour in the moonlight. So do robins, song sparrows and ovenbirds, to name a few more.

When I was small, night was something forbidding, mysterious, indefinably evil. Now I find it infinitely more intriguing, though still mysterious and exciting. Alison and I have sat on a log at the edge of our Christmas-tree woods, listening to sowbugs and centipedes poking along in the leaf mold. We have heard the scream of a rabbit in the talons of a barred owl. We've heard the click of a bat as it snatched an insect in full flight. And we've chuckled at the agitated whispers of the deer mice as they discussed these two motionless bumps on their log.

At night we can hear the many little sounds that are usually swallowed up in daytime's hubbub. A whole new world, too, is afield, afoot and a-wing. The sound of an earthworm pulling leaves into its burrow becomes enormously important. The scent of a distant skunk, the tracery of violets on the air, add a wild backdrop to a land where a sudden sound or sight may still bring the hackles up along the back of my neck— even if it's no more than a couple of frogs in a swamp.

SUMMER

CHAPTER NINE

Pokey

HE CAME running to us after he had lost his mother in a forest fire. We didn't want anything to do with him. We could see hundreds of sharp little needles underneath his black fur. But the ashes of the fire were still smoking, and he cried aloud as his scorched feet made little puffs of dust.

Warner Pierce, a neighbor boy, scooped him up with a shovel. At once the little porcupine balled up into a silent mass of prickers. Tom pulled off his cloth jacket and held it like a net while Warner dumped the baby into it. Then, wadding it loosely, we carried the tiny orphan to the car.

"Well," Tom said as we unwrapped the bundle on the back seat, "what on earth are we going to do with him?"

We've spent more than a year searching for the answer to that question, and we haven't really found it yet.

The first thing, however, was to get some food into the little fellow. We recalled seeing beech and fir trees debarked by porcupines, so we gathered some of the branches. But the little quill-pig was too frightened to eat. All that day and evening he just huddled in the corner of a box.

When he still hadn't eaten the next morning, we decided to give him the universal food welcomed by all mammal babies—warm milk. I put on a heavy leather jacket and gloves, and picked him up.

Holding him on his back, I poked at his mouth with a medicine dropper. His long curved black claws were drawn together as a shield over his dark little nose. His black eyes were tightly shut. Plainly he expected this to be his last moment on earth.

But the instant I touched his lips with the sweetened milk his resistance collapsed. Opening his eyes, he seized the dropper and pulled at it until the milk was gone. Then a pink tongue appeared for a moment and licked his lips.

That warm milk did wonders for his attitude toward life. His pincushion armor relaxed, until he became astonishingly small—no larger than your doubled fist. In less than an hour he was exploring the kitchen floor. In two days he was so tame that I put away my leather jacket. He has never bristled at any of us since.

"What'll we call him?" asked Tom.

I had been reading Thornton Burgess stories to Roger as a bedtime treat. We had met Blacky the Crow, Peter Rabbit,

Jimmy Skunk and Prickly Porky. "Porky," suggested Roger. "But it's too bad he isn't a little bear cub. Then we could call him 'Smokey,' like the bear who lost his mother in a fire."

"How about combining the two," asked Janice, "and making it 'Pokey'?"

Nobody knew then how fast or slow he could run. But after seeing him at top speed, we decided that "Pokey" was a good name all round. His gallop might get him a mile in a couple of hours. But it lasts only ten or twelve feet at a stretch. The rest of the time he noses along at his customary amble, which is about one third as fast as a human's leisurely walk.

From the first, he jumped at every sound. Although his ears are so short that they're hidden in the fur of his round head, they're surprisingly keen. Probably they make up for eyesight that lets him see only three or four feet. While I was feeding him one evening, Peg was mending in the next room. Pokey was murmuring contentedly as he downed his rations. Then Peg dropped a button on the floor. At the sharp sound his quills came to full alert. He half-whirled to meet his unseen enemy. Even in the warm kitchen, with the soothing taste of sweetened milk, he couldn't forget that he was a wild creature.

"How does a porcupine play?" Janice asked one evening as she was doing a high-school report on our pet. "Does he chase his tail like a kitten?"

This tickled Roger. "Think what'd happen if he ever *caught* it!"

A few days later Janice's question was answered. Alison had just finished feeding Pokey in the kitchen. Suddenly she cried out in alarm. "Mother! Daddy! Come quick!"

When we got to the kitchen, she was standing in a corner. "Something's the matter with Pokey!"

He was doing a war dance. That's the only way you could

describe it. With his back in an exaggerated arch like that of a cat on the Hallowe'en designs, every quill raised, he whirled as if on a pivot. Four or five turns one way, four or five the other. Then straight backward, at a run, bristle-tail swinging like a scythe. A couple of sideways hops, stiff-legged, then back into the spin again.

Around the kitchen he went. Every time he slowed down we'd stamp our feet and start him up again. I've never seen a porcupine in full action against an enemy, but this must have been Pokey's way of rehearsal. After watching him we decided there's only one thing as prickly as an angry porcupine. And that's a playful one.

One day Peg took Pokey to a teachers' meeting. Little ham actor that he is, he obligingly went through his spin for the delighted audience. But the best was yet to come. When they all sang "America" as part of their closing exercise, Pokey sat up and put his paws against his ears. All through the song he swayed from side to side and squinted his eyes in pain.

The last verse collapsed in pandemonium.

By the time he was two months old, he had graduated to cereal, crackers, green leaves and potato chips. Our baby was growing up—in more ways than one. This was evident one night when Peg woke up. "Ps-s-st!" she whispered. "What's that?"

We listened in the dark. Scrape, scrape. Then a pause. Scrape, scrape again.

"Mice," I suggested hopefully.

Peg snorted. "That's no mouse. That's a porcupine. And ten to one he's helping himself to our furniture."

When we got downstairs and flipped the light switch, Pokey blinked pleasantly at us from the top of the kitchen table. He'd tipped the butter over and helped himself. He'd taken several gouges out of a bowl of apples. Now he was nibbling at the table edge—tablecloth and all—as if it were an ear of corn. Squealing with pleasure, he ran across the table to greet us.

The next morning we asked the children what should be done with him.

"We can't let him go in the woods," Alison protested. "He'd walk up to the first hunter he saw."

"Besides," Tom added, "he's not even afraid of dogs. He wouldn't know how to protect himself."

It was probably true. Pokey got along fine with Jack, our big shepherd dog. He kept those murderous daggers covered as they played together. He loved to crawl up Jack's heavy fur and ride on his back. I could imagine just how long he'd last if he met a hound in the woods. By the time he found out the dog's intentions, it would be too late.

I helpfully suggested putting him in a zoo. They looked at me, shocked. Put our own porcupine in a common zoo?

So I got some wire and made him a cage. But Pokey wanted none of it. Before, he had whimpered a bit when he'd been cramped or restrained. Now he became vociferous.

Climbing up on the roof-wire of his cage, he shouted his protest. First he tried a hoo-hoo-hoo, sounding like a barking dog. Then a petulant squeal. Then a mournful wail, like a hungry baby. Finally he subsided into a hurt little sniffle, as if to let us know that the cage was giving him pneumonia.

He complained all night long, but we didn't give in. He's been in the cage ever since, though the moral victory is his. Somebody usually takes him out every few hours. He's just too much fun to let alone.

I used to let him ride my typewriter carriage, for instance, until he became too big. He still shuffles into my study when he hears it going, and climbs up on my lap hopefully. I put him back down on the floor, but he shinnies right back. Then I have to call for someone to rescue me.

Pokey loves to play tag, too, as long as he can be It. He runs after us as fast as his short legs can carry him. As soon as he catches one of us, someone else will stamp his feet and Pokey will gallop after him.

A local forester heard about our strange pet and came to see for himself. "Porcupines," he told me as he watched Pokey chase the children on the lawn, "never play tag. They are completely antisocial, stupid, destructive and uninteresting. That's what we were told in forestry school. Obviously, your porcupine has never been to school."

No matter where he is, Pokey responds at once to his name. We often put him in a tree to exercise his claws and keep his rodent teeth worn down. When we want him again, we merely speak to him. Sampling the air with nose and ears, he decides exactly where we are, even if his myopic eyes cannot pick us out. Then he faithfully hunches backward down the limb, his teeth chattering in anticipation, feeling along with his sensitive muscular tail. Once in our arms, he gently nibbles at a wrist or finger, as if to tell us how glad he is to be back again.

His feet are marvelous tools. Armed with four long crescent-shaped claws in front, five in the rear, they are flat and black, like little thumbless monkey hands. They can get a surprising grip on a branch. And so strongly hooked are the claws that he can walk along while hanging like a sloth upside down under a branch.

Pokey walks flat-footed, like a little bear. When he's really going somewhere, he carries his tail tilted almost straight up. Often he walks a few steps on his hind legs, using the tail as the third point of a tripod. With his heavy gray coat of fur and quills, extending right to his hands and feet, he reminds Peg of a foot-high little man in a snowsuit.

Can Pokey throw his quills? Actually, he cannot. But, in effect, he can. Once, in his war dance, he slapped his tail against a chair leg. A few quills snapped loose and flew across the room. But ordinarily you'd have to touch a porky to get even a single quill. The spines of full-grown adults—four inches or longer—stay with their owner until some foolhardy creature rams against their tiny barbed points and leaps back with a few dozen.

The porcupine merely grows new quills to replace those he lost. Meantime, the backward-pointing barbs cause the quills to work steadily deeper in his attacker. Once they have caught hold, they move in one direction only—inward.

However, we don't even worry about his quills. We always pick Pokey up by putting our hands beneath him. His belly is as soft as a spaniel's ear, for its hairs have not differentiated into the slender white shafts which cover the rest of his body from nose to tail. It's the belly that is sought out by the fisher-cat, large cousin of the weasel, and the porcupine's only effective natural enemy.

People ask me how I think such a prickly baby can be born without hurting the mother. Probably the answer lies in the softening effect of water on the baby quills. Soaked in its own natal fluid, the single newborn porcupine must be no more spiny than a pound of wet sawdust. And, like a puppy, it's encased in a membrane when born, offering the mother further protection.

The mechanics of mating in such spiny creatures has interested me. I'm told, however, that it's an essentially normal process. As porcupines can hold their quills flat against the body when necessary, mating poses no great problem. We have quite a number of wild porcupines here in the Green Mountains of Vermont. Perhaps next autumn I'll find a wild one, release Pokey near it, and note the process for myself. Half a year old, he weighs about five pounds, so we figure he is about half grown. He's so durable, according to my books, that we can expect him to live about ten years.

Although we love our pincushion pet, we know that if he'd grown up in the wild he would have lived on something besides whole-wheat bread and fig bars. I've seen trees girdled by porcupines—useless, stunted things with their tops dead and with disease spreading from gnawing injury. The forester told me that some timber stands may be rendered almost 100 percent worthless by porky damage.

"But we've brought it on ourselves," he added. "That fisher-cat used to be a wonderful control on the porcupine until we killed it off for its fur. Now with the fisher gone and abandoned farms springing up to nice tender saplings, the porcupines have things their own way."

"Why can't we bring back the fishers, then?"

"We're trying. It's worked in Maine, New York and elsewhere. We hope it works in Vermont, too. Meantime, we've got a big problem."

He and I were watching Pokey as he nibbled at the greenery in our sugar maple. "How many acres did you say were lost in the forest fire that orphaned Pokey?" he asked.

"They figured about sixty."

"And some of it was standing timber ready for harvest?"

"About twenty acres of good trees."

He picked up a leaf that had just fluttered down from my busy pet in the tree above. "It'd take a lot of porcupines to equal the damage done by a single match, wouldn't it, Ron?"

CHAPTER TEN

Stump City

IF I COULD choose but a
quarter-mile of land for my own, I would make sure that it
contained an old stump.

Inch for inch, I believe such an area to be more fascinating
than any other spot on my hundred acres.

To look at it from a distance, you'd not think it was much at
all. Just an old hollow tree, it seems, a few feet tall, with
perhaps some plants and stones at its base. Even if you walk
closer, the rugged features of its trunk hardly beckon you to
stay awhile. Yet as a boy I've spent full afternoons around

such a spot, learning new facts by the hour. And I hope I'll yet be able to enjoy many more, with the stump as my teacher.

There was the time the children discovered the *Ichneumons,* for instance. I could tell that something was up when Roger and Alison began to whisper together. When they started toward the woods, my curiosity was aroused.

"What's the matter, kids?"

"Nothing," said Alison, though her sober face belied her words.

"Well, there must be something wrong. What are you going up into the woods for?"

"Alison wanted me to see something," said Roger.

"Like what, for instance?"

"Like a wasp that tried to sting a tree and got caught and now it's stuck and I don't know what to do. . . ." Alison's voice trailed off as she anxiously watched for my reaction.

Tender-hearted little Sunny would struggle five minutes to open a window, just to let out a fly that was buzzing against the glass. Once she brought in a bird's egg that had been broken, tears streaming down her face. Our pasture has a small grave-yard containing mice, rabbits, sparrows, surmounted by loving little wooden crosses. Now she was upset over the fate of a wasp.

"Tried to sting a tree?" I puzzled. "What do you mean?"

"Golly, I don't know. Oh, Daddy, do you have time to come and help it?"

The summer air beckoned more than my noisy typewriter, so I followed her out into the sunlight. We went up to the edge of my woods. Alison led us to a dying maple. Its bark was half gone and great woodpecker-holes stared out of it like sightless eyes.

"Right there," she said. Not one, but three large yellow-and-brown wasps had taken their positions on the bark. Two of them strained with bent backs like little workmen. They thrust against long threadlike objects, or ovipositors, projecting from their abdomens.

I had read about these insects. Now I had a chance to watch them firsthand. They were Ichneumon wasps, intent on penetrating the tunnels of borers deep in the wood.

"Don't worry, Alison," I assured her. "They're not trapped." I told her what I knew about the wasps.

We watched as they drove their slender drills deeper into the tree. Each drill was coiled in a membrane of the insect's abdomen. It seemed to be about four inches long. With each pulsation of the wasp's body, the tiny lance forced its way further toward the unseen victim. Then, when the burrow was reached, an egg would be sent down the hollow shaft of the lance. Soon the little wasp grub would feed on its wood-boring host.

I tried to shoo one wasp away but, though it buzzed its wings, it was anchored fast by that ovipositor. Like the wolf spider drumming on leaves—indeed, like many creatures absorbed in the art of reproduction—it was exposing itself to danger for the preservation of the race.

"How does the wasp know for sure it'll hit a wood-borer's hole?" asked Roger.

His question was answered, at least in part, by the third wasp. Slowly it went over the surface of the stump, tapping and feeling it with its antennae. They reminded me of two little fingers, "walking" delicately along, now stopping to explore some likely spot and now taking random samples every half-inch.

Finally the wasp stopped at a certain point. To us it looked no different from the rest of the tree. Perhaps the tapping had detected a hollow echo from the hidden burrow. Perhaps the exquisite sense of smell of those antennae had indicated that this would be a good place. At any rate, she settled down and began to drill.

We watched her for the better part of an hour. As near as I could see she was hardly half through by that time, to judge by the length of ovipositor still showing.

Peg called us for lunch. As we started away, Alison took one last backward look. "Golly, all that work just to lay an egg. What if she misses? Then she has to do it all over again."

Roger chuckled. "Sure. But what hurry is a wasp in?"

When we remembered to go back to the stump several days later the wasps, of course, were gone. The woodpeckers had deepened their own holes—perhaps in search of the same borers sought by the wasps. The one living branch on the side of the stump had a piece of bark hanging loosely. When I pulled at it, it was not bark at all, but the soft body and wings of a hawk moth, perfectly camouflaged against its gray-white surroundings.

Startled, I dropped it. As it flew away, bright markings of the orange underwings flashed in the sunlight. An oriole dived down to snatch it, but before it got there the moth clapped up against another tree trunk and disappeared again.

Puzzled, the oriole flew back to its perch. The moth, perfectly matching the grizzled bark, had hidden itself in plain sight. I was reminded of my friends who had wondered where to find a maple tree when they were standing right in the shade of one. Maples and moths, I've discovered, are like many things of nature—they're there for the looking.

Sooner or later, if you look long enough, you'll find evidence of nearly every terrestrial group in the animal kingdom around a dead or dying tree. A zoologist friend of mine has collected over one hundred fifty separate species of insects alone from a pine stump on his college campus.

Peel off the bark of a stump and you may see the fantastic tracery of the bark beetles. Their tunnels fan out from a central area where the eggs were laid. Take a magnifying glass, and you'll see the tiny spotted or striped mites, tigers of their own little world, looking for small insects. If you break open a chunk of the wood you may find it honeycombed with the galleries made by the large black carpenter ant. Sow bugs, distant relatives of the crab and lobster, trot placidly along on their many legs like their domestic namesakes. Centipedes and millipedes wend through the dampness like little freight trains.

There are even cockroaches. These irrepressible garbagemen, whose ancestors were among the first of all insects some 300 million years ago, scoot over the tree roots in search of anything edible. Often we see their built-in babysitter—the egg case which the female carries until it is nearly ready to hatch.

The little roaches, looking much like their parents, often travel with them for weeks or months after hatching. Since mother roach may have several successive broods during this time, the entire clan is a living family tree. I've seen a mother, father, what appeared to be married sons and daughters, and an assortment of juniors ranging down to the baby—or, in this case, babies.

One time I watched a bulldozer clearing land for a house. As it pushed over an old stump, a cloud of insects arose. The cloud drifted upward a moment, then settled on the operator of the machine. He slapped frantically and vaulted out of his seat. Luckily they were not the swarm of bees that he probably expected. They were nothing but termites, whose winged virgin males and females had been waiting in the hidden wooden galleries for their mating flight.

There were several thousand of these "reproductives," as they are called, attended by thousands more of the wingless, blind, milk-white workers. To fulfill its destiny, each reproductive would launch into the air—a foot or a mile, it hardly mattered which, as long as it flew—and flutter to earth again. Then, together with its mate, it would break off those gauzy wings and tunnel back underground. Leaving the sunlight forever, the honeymoon pair would begin a new termite colony.

"Termite kings and queens may be the longest-lived of all insects," a museum staff member once told me. "Some tropical types may live thirty or forty years—perhaps longer."

Like the wood roaches, termites are powerless to digest the cellulose of sound, undecayed wood. They have to depend on little partners which live within their bodies. We saw them under the museum's microscope. They were tiny protozoans, each looking like a fuzzy pear. In return for the shelter provided by the termite, they break down cellulose to the point where it can be utilized by the insect. A termite without its little tenants will still eat wood, but it soon starves.

On a July afternoon I was hiking with some Boy Scouts on the Long Trail. A group had gone on ahead, but suddenly stopped and began to examine something at the base of a dead tree. At first glance it seemed to be the droppings of some kind of animal.

"Fox," theorized one Scout.

"Skunk," said another.

They looked at me. "What kind of animal made this, Mr. Rood?"

I was on the spot. Then a noise above our heads came to my rescue. We glanced up and saw a large hole in the tree.

"Something's in there," said one of the boys in a low voice.

He took a stick to whack against the tree. At the same instant I realized what had made the droppings. On a hunch, I told the boys to sit down quietly. After a few minutes I had one of them go softly to the tree and scratch on the bark.

The results were immediate. A gray-brown head appeared at the entrance to the hole. Two yellow eyes with great black pupils glared at us. Beneath these a strong hooked beak snapped a warning.

The face disappeared. "Was that an owl?" someone asked.

"Sure was," spoke Bill Little, the troop's bird-watcher. "The biggest of 'em all—a great horned owl."

We stood looking at the hole; then he bent over and poked at the droppings. "And these here are his pellets."

Carefully we pulled the gray masses of fur and bones apart. We identified portions of the rib of some small animal, and fur like that of a cottontail rabbit. There was a mouse skull, shrew skull, and several small bones. In accepted owl fashion, he had swallowed his prey, hair and all. Later his stomach had rolled the indigestible matter into soft pellets and regurgitated them. Odorless, dry, they are often a clue as to whether a hollow tree is inhabited. Sometimes, however, like my chickadee carrying away the waste from its nest, the owl flies away with the pellets so as to leave no telltale sign.

Sometimes bats are found sleeping in hollow trees. Once three raccoons peered inquisitively out when I scratched on the bark. A friend of mine once flushed a bobcat the same way in the woods. The list of creatures known to use the hollow of an old stump would read like a *Who's Who of the Woods.*

The deadwood bonanza, however, gives way to the living. There was a stump near a camp in Connecticut where we used to visit friends. One night as we left them to start homeward, we saw a strange glow in the woods. It looked like a patch of dim moonlight, although the night was dark.

Curious, we investigated. It came directly from the wood of the stump. We picked up a piece of it. It glowed with a cold greenish light in our hands. Kicking at the stump, my brother discovered more of it. So we staged an impromptu battle, tossing fiery chunks back and forth in the dark.

Later I learned that phosphorescent wood, or "fox fire," is really the work of a fungus. It infiltrates the tissues of the dead stump, aiding in its decay and the return of nutrients to the soil. It works along with a host of bacteria, other fungi, molds, lichens and roundworms.

We owe our lives to scavengers. Without them, all the material taken from the soil, the air and water would eventually be locked in the dead bodies of countless animals and plants. Animals raised in germ-free laboratories do not decay after death. They just lie there until they are dried mummies.

It would be handy for a paleontologist if mummy dinosaurs and coal-age plants were still lying around to be identified. However, with vital materials uselessly bound in their bodies, there wouldn't be much left to make a paleontologist.

I'll never learn the last thing—in fact, hardly the first—about the life of the stump city. Just the other day Peg read to me that there's almost no such thing as a dead stump. For, even if the main portion dies, the roots go on and on through the soil, perhaps sending up a shoot fifty feet away from the parent tree, and fifty years removed.

Hence the little red maple sapling which grows thirty feet from the red maple stump in my back yard could well be older —if you count the roots—than the gnarled butternut giant which shades it.

CHAPTER ELEVEN

Watery World

"SEE WHAT I mean, Dad? It's not hard for a fish to see in those bubbles at all."

I nodded and ducked beneath the water again. Tom and I had wondered how a brook trout could possibly see a worm in the tumbling, racing water of our river rapids. So we had donned face-masks and snorkels and invaded their world to see for ourselves.

The answer was quite simple. The churning rapids look opaque and white to us as we stand on the bank. But seen from a fish's-eye viewpoint, there's a lot of water in between the

93

bubbles. I sneaked up behind an eight-incher, its nose pointed upstream, its tail fanning the water as it kept its position against the current or ranged from side to side. Lying low along the bottom, it was beneath most of the bubbles. Now and then it rose to investigate a bit of debris that went racing by.

Tom was above me in the next rapids. He must have disturbed a large stone, for the water was suddenly filled with little creatures. They had been dislodged from their homes and now tumbled along to the waiting trout. I was reminded of two fish biologists who had once investigated our river. They spread a fine net across the stream. Then they overturned stones in the water above it. Within ten minutes the net was black with creatures I hardly knew existed.

We love to snorkel-ize in our river, Tom and I. The rapids are just as interesting as the crystal depths of the old swimming hole down by the bridge. We must look rather bizarre as we crawl along with our backs awash in a foot of water, but the world we have entered is even more bizarre.

There are no sharks or barracudas to make our skin-deep skin-diving a TV thriller. The largest denizen of our watery world is a twenty-pound beaver. Three years ago he took up residence in the riverbank. Next in size comes a snapping turtle of about ten pounds which once greeted me under a watery ledge. It must have scratched its way up from Lake Champlain or some swampy area a few miles downstream. Add to this the mink we saw last winter on the ice, an occasional muskrat and a rare otter, and you have nearly all the large vertebrates of our New Haven River.

Yet the little creatures make up in interest what they lack in size. Some of them that tumbled down the rapids from Tom to me that day were caddis worms, those strange creatures which build their own little underwater homes.

We often find these insects in our first examination of the stomachs of trout in May. We like to analyze the contents to find out what these fish have been eating. One time we were investigating Roger's first trout of the season, a fine eight-and-a-half-incher.

"Dad," Roger asked as he indicated a mass of sand and twigs, "how come this trout eats only sticks and stones?"

It didn't make sense to me. "I don't know, Roger. Better look again and see if there isn't something else, too."

He poked around for a moment. Then I could almost see a question mark form above his head like a character in a comic strip. "How come, Dad? How come there are little worms living inside those sand grains?"

We prodded some more until we got a perfect specimen. It was a caddis worm, the larva of a brown mothlike fly. Soft as a caterpillar, it had made a protecting house of sand grains glued together. Other caddis worms had used tiny twigs. We've often seen them crawling along on rocks in the swiftest water, clinging with their six sprawly legs. Their elongated cases streamed out behind them in the current.

Strange, almost fantastic, are the ways employed by water creatures to resist the current and make a living at the same time. Beetle larvae as round and as flat as a penny cling like olive-drab paint spots to the rocks. We used to collect these "water-pennies" as children. Fresh-water limpets—little snails with shallow shells like tiny overturned saucers—stick to the smooth stones. They cling so tightly that you may break a fingernail in prying them loose. Brook sculpins—strange little brown fish with large heads, toadlike mouths and fins which they can dig into the sand—dart a few inches and then rest on the bottom, securely anchored by those fins. Diving spiders spin little webs which entrap air bubbles, thus affording an

95

underwater breathing chamber. Flat stone-fly nymphs scuttle over the rocks like fiddler crabs on a beach.

In our study of trout stomachs a new insect suddenly shows up as May becomes June. This is the mayfly, a delicate creature whose story is one of the most touching in nature.

It begins with the tiny young which hatch out from eggs left in the water by their mother. Flattened so as to crawl over the surface of rocks in the current, they are yet marvelously flexible, and some species can dart through still water like a minnow. The stream races past feathery gills along their sides, supplying them with oxygen at no effort.

All summer they creep on the bottom or swim through the water. They feed on algae, decaying leaves or other vegetation. They need their streamlined shapes and neutral colors, for they have many enemies. Should the current snatch them out of hiding, they will be snapped up by predatory water beetles, salamanders and water scorpions. Nearly every fish eagerly awaits them. I have only to disturb a few pebbles to bring the dace and minnows in an underwater swarm.

Some mayfly species spend but a single precarious summer this way. Others continue for a second or even a third summer. Three years is a long time for an insect to live. But one day they quit their juvenile haunts and climb out on sticks and bushes along the shore.

Now the somber naiad bursts its skin. In its place is a winged creature as light as river foam. And well it might be, for its fragile body contains a bubble of air. It has done all its feeding as a naiad. Now the digestive system becomes inflated with air. Even the new mouthparts are incomplete. It will eat no more.

We often watch these delicate creatures in this moment of triumph. For it is also a moment of tragedy. Chattering birds swoop low and pick them off even as they rest on the discarded juvenile skin. Trout leap out of the water to snatch them. So important are the mayflies to trout that they have engendered the art of dry-fly fishing. This was ruefully described by a fisherman with an empty creel. "Fly fishing," he said, "is the offering of an imitation mayfly to an imaginary trout."

Like a prospective bride trying on wedding gowns, the mayfly molts again—sometimes even a third time. Alone among a million or more insects, it is the only one that sheds its jacket in the winged state. Fully adult at last, it launches into the air.

Sometimes I can follow the entire rest of its life from my perch on our bridge railing. It is astonishingly short. It meets one of the millions of its kind that has emerged the same day, and it joins with it in the only companionship it knows—the cold togetherness of an insect mating. Then, hours or minutes later—if some sharp-eyed bird has not found the pair—their lives come to an end.

The male falls dying to the ground. The female, pressed with her mission, descends to the water. Sometimes her eggs force their way out in a stringy mass, and she merely washes them off by dipping her abdomen in the stream. Other times she folds her wings tightly, enclosing a bubble of air with them. Then she makes her way to the underwater stones to deposit her eggs. Still other times her waning strength barely allows her to fly over water and drop helplessly to the surface. There, as her body is buffeted and torn in the rapids, the eggs are at last set free.

The entire adult life of my mayfly neighbors may encompass less than the time between my breakfast and lunch. Some species may live several days, but this is still in sharp contrast to the naiad life of perhaps three years. Small wonder that Aristotle and all who have followed him call them by the name *Ephemerida*. For they are the ephemeral ones, living but a day.

Besides the mayfly naiads, we sometimes meet another swimmer, this one equipped with a snorkel. It's the fearsome water scorpion, *Nepa apiculata*. Fearsome, that is, if you're a minnow. Actually it's about three quarters of an inch long and quite afraid of humans. Its muscular front legs are strongly hooked, with an action like a pair of ice tongs. They hug its prey while the powerful beak stabs and drinks its body fluids. At its rear is a breathing tube half as long as the body. This projects into the air as the creature hangs just beneath the surface or clings to a rock. Then, head downward and tongs spread, it waits for a victim.

One time, on an alder branch that dipped down into a still pool, we found *Ranatra,* leggy cousin of the water scorpion. It looked like a slender, somewhat larger, edition of the same bug, complete with snorkel. What startled us, however, was its voice. It "talked" by shrugging its shoulders. Roughened areas at the base of its legs rubbed against its body and made a distinct squeak. It squeaked twice at me as it was sunning on the alder branch. When I alarmed it, it fled beneath the water, still squeaking b-z-z-zt! b-z-z-zt!

My favorite, however, is that insufferable bounder, the buffalo gnat, or black fly. As an adult it outranks even the notorious Jersey mosquito, for its several varieties may begin biting in May and continue to July as new species emerge from the water. As a larva, however, it has my unfeigned admiration.

We often come across hundreds of them in our underwater trips. Like other fly larvae, they are maggots. They often occur in such numbers as to make the surface of stones appear to be covered with moss. Unlike many other maggots, however, they catch their food in nets.

Little suction cups fore and aft allow them to cling to the rock or to a silken line which they lay down with their mouths.

Their head is surrounded by a crown of spines so as to act as a netlike funnel to catch tiny organisms floating in the water. Thus when the black fly maggot is in position, with its funnel-head pointed upstream, it's a regular little fisherman, complete with silk line and net.

The portion of their lives that amazes me most, however, is that fraction between babyhood and maturity. The pupa or cocoon is spun by the larva right on the underwater rock. When it comes time for the adult to emerge, it rises in a tiny bubble of air. Careening along through the rapids in its filmy prison, it quickly reaches the surface. The bubble bursts—and in that split second before its wings get wet, the fly rises in full flight.

Last year four friends of mine went up into the northern wilds for a week of fishing. They were back in two days. "Those cussed black flies," moaned one of them through puffy lips, "they were everywhere. They bit like fire. We couldn't begin to get out on the river without slathering on the bug repellant. The humpbacked little beggars got in our hair, food, blankets, car, luggage.

"They sang us to sleep and met us at breakfast," he continued. "We might have stuck it out for the rest of the week, but the water was too high for good fishing, anyway. So we left the whole blooming river to the black flies."

I recalled one time I had to sleep in the Adirondacks with the car windows rolled up tight to escape from their torment. Wildlife men tell me that they'll actually drain the blood from a nesting bird or a hiding fawn.

Small wonder that scientists have given these little creatures such names as *Simulium molestum*, the molester; *Simulium irritatum*, the irritator, and *Simulium tribulatum*, the tribulator.

I like best, however, the scientific epithet spat out at a certain tropical black fly. It's just about the climax in scientific name-calling. You'll find it soberly printed in sedate zoological literature.

Its name? *Simulium damnosum.*

CHAPTER TWELVE

Grass Menagerie

TOM held the thermometer. I kept my eyes glued to the watch. Peg and the girls did the counting. Roger wrote down the results.

The object of this family experiment was to find the temperature by listening to cricket-chirps in the meadow.

Our snowy tree cricket, like other insects, lives his life faster or slower depending on the temperature. "Raise the Fahrenheit," as Roger says, and he'll eat, move and sing faster. Looking at it from the other way round, the faster he's singing, the hotter it must be. Count the high, trilling chirps of *Oecanthus niveus* for fifteen seconds, add forty, and you'll come within a degree or two of the reading on the thermometer.

"Thirty-two chirps," said Janice when I called the fifteen-second mark.

Roger wrote it down on his paper and busied himself with the pencil for a moment. Then, triumphantly: "It should be seventy-two degrees."

Tom looked at his thermometer. "The mercury reads seventy-one. Wow, Dad! Almost perfect!"

We tiptoed closer to this little songster with the built-in thermostat. Although he usually sings during the night, this was a cloudy day. In his exuberance he didn't seem to know the difference between clouds and darkness.

Finally we discovered him on a goldenrod. His pale green-white body was half an inch long and his glassy-clear wings were raised as sound-organs. We could see them vibrate with each chirp as they scraped back and forth on each other.

We inched closer. I clumsily pressed against the goldenrod. Instantly the cricket stopped. But, amazingly, the song kept going. For Oecanthus is the choirmaster's dream: he sings in perfect timing with other males in the vicinity. It sounds like just one song. Although our cricket had quit temporarily, perhaps a dozen others kept up the tempo. When he joined in again, it was right in time with the chorus.

I've driven along roadways when a whole fencerow seemed to be throbbing with the tree cricket's song. Even at sixty miles per hour, you hear just the same note, repeated over and over as you pass one cricket orchestra after another.

This is just one item in his bag of tricks. Although he can hear the notes of other males by means of "ears" on his front legs, his slender mate is apparently stone deaf. So all that insistent singing is lost on her. But she comes anyway. A little scent-packet on his body is uncovered when he raises those wings, and its fragrance is wafted to his intended bride. Hopping and flying upwind, she makes her way to his side. If she then nibbles at the gland itself, his conquest is complete.

We wondered why the cricket bothered to sing if his lady couldn't hear him. So we tried an experiment. A certain tree cricket was on one side of a fencepost. We placed another on the opposite side of the same post. Carefully backing away, we settled down to watch.

Everything was quiet until one started to chirp. Instantly the attitude of the other changed. He raised his wings and chirped (in unison, of course) too, but quietly sneaked around the post as he did so.

Soon the two were facing each other, apparently getting madder by the minute. Somehow it reminded me of a couple of sopranos I once heard in a little church choir—each trying to outdo the other.

Finally they were touching their long antennae, like fencers crossing swords preparatory to the duel. There was a sudden flurry of insect bodies. Then one cricket leaped away in long half-flying arcs. The other, victorious, rejoined the chorus around him.

Thus we were able to guess one meaning of the tree cricket's chirp. Like the robin's carol, the bull elk's bugle, and a lawn sign that says "The Joneses live here," it was a declaration of territory. Just as Mr. Jones will allow a dog, a cat and a few birds to share his nest, but no other Mr. Joneses, so *Oecanthus niveus* tolerates moths, katydids and leaf hoppers, but no other O. niveus—except, of course, his mate.

Often when I consider the many kinds of creatures in my

103

meadow, each with its own little world, I'm reminded of an atlas of North America. One page shows the mountains and deserts, another the states and provinces. Still another shows the rivers and lakes, another the principal railroads, and so on. But they're all North America.

So it is with my meadow. The tree cricket keeps pretty well to tall weeds in the meadow or to bushes along its edge. Hence a tree-cricket map would show the meadow as a relatively hollow square with the sides denser than the center. The same meadow mapped for bobolinks would tend to be all center and no sides, for the bobolink delights in nesting in the tall grass out in the open. Meadow mice would be mapped in fine checkerboard fashion, each square standing for the few square yards' home range of this species. Jumping mice might appear as a giant gingham print, for these long-tailed creatures are less common and need a larger territory for their six-foot leaps. Even deer would show up here and there in summer, for they often come out onto the meadow's edge at dusk for weeds and clover.

Mapping the smaller creatures, however, would be almost impossible. For many, a single plant may be all the territory they need. One summer day after a picnic I lay in the grass watching a softball game. My attention was attracted by the actions of a blade of grass two feet in front of me. It would bend down and then snap up, almost like the pole of a fisherman getting a bite.

The sun glinted on a strand of silk, and my wiggling grass was explained. The silk was the anchor line of a garden spider's web. Every time the handsome black-and-gold creature moved in repairing a tear in the web, the grass nodded in reply. As it nodded it gave a little twitch to some fifty or more aphids perched halfway up the stem. Riding herd on these were half a dozen ants, stroking them for the sticky-sweet material given off by their bodies. Beneath the soil, I knew, were more aphid "cows" feeding on roots and being milked by unseen ant farmers.

On a neighboring plant was a little green caterpillar, cutting away at the edge of a grass leaf like a tiny pair of shears. As I watched, a stiletto bug stalked up on slender legs and thrust its beak into the caterpillar. The little victim twisted its hardest, but the beak held firm. Five minutes later the bug dropped the empty husk of its meal and climbed over to the next leaf.

Other plants around me supported still other little tenants. Bees hummed in the clover. Yellow crab spiders lurked in buttercup blossoms. I dipped into the bubble bath of a frog-hopper and pulled out the squat green insect. Placing it on another plant, I watched as it inserted its beak into the stem. Soon it began to form little bubbles at the tail end of its body, like a tiny bubble-pipe. Shortly it was covered again with a house of bubbles half as big as a marble. "Frog spit," we children used to call it, never once suspecting that it was made by a relative of the aphids and not by a frog at all.

"You're out!" the umpire called, and the game was over.

As I got up and strode through the grass, leaf hoppers and grasshoppers leaped in every direction. A single swish of an entomologist's net may garner a hundred or more of the former, a dozen or more of the latter. My own record with a twelve-inch net is twenty-one grasshoppers in a single swoop.

In my days as an Air Force pilot I used to look down from the sky at little villages and towns. Although they were laid out in streets, fields and parkways, not a sign of life was visible. Yet I knew that if I were to draw closer I'd find hundreds of beings—dogs, cats, people, mice, birds—in even the smallest hamlet. This is the way I feel when I walk idly through a meadow. There are so many thousands of little lives going on below me.

Many of these are visible to anyone who wants to lie on his stomach in the summer sun and squint through a magnifying glass at the world of grass roots. Every sand grain becomes a boulder, every weed a tree, and every insect a six-legged dragon. The great French scientist J. Henri Fabre made many of the observations which gained him world acclaim—and nearly the lockup as well for such unstately procedure—while on his knees in the grass, peering at an ant or grasshopper.

Perhaps it's less than dignified to meet the meadow creatures at their own level, but it's rewarding nevertheless. A couple of ants pulling at a dead spider can absorb you for an hour. Sometimes in their haste to get the prey home they pull in opposite directions. Other times, one may get on top and tug uselessly while the other has to haul the combined weight.

You may find a meadow slug, that soft, shell-less snail which can creep along a razor's edge with safety. Its sensitive probings are fascinating as it lays down a trail of mucus and glides on this frictionless bed—even over a patch of sand. An eight-eyed jumping spider, gruesome enough for any ten-year-old's comic books, leaps twenty times its length to capture a gnat. A Daddy-long-legs, or harvestman, stalks over the scene, somehow not quite able to preserve his dignity with eight or ten little red mites running over his body like small hitch-hikers.

At this level, your ears serve you as well as your eyes. Sometimes, with certain species of ants, you can hear a tiny piping, like a thin little squeak. Not many people know that some ants can sing, but the noise is made by scraping two abdominal segments together. You may well discover singing beetles, too, of which there are many kinds, as well as singing wasps and even grubs.

You may hear the whisper of a box turtle, too. This sound is made as it exhales its breath when you startle it. By deflating its lungs, it makes room for its legs in the shell as it withdraws inside its bony armor.

You will probably witness the ecstasy of mating, the tragedy of death. Once I watched the last struggles of a dying cricket. It scuttled around at my feet in such a strange manner that I bent down to look at it. Nothing seemed physically wrong except that it was unusually swollen. But then as I watched, a grayish-white thread poked out of a chink in its segmented body. To my astonishment, the thread grew and grew. It twisted and bent, becoming longer and longer, until nearly six inches of it writhed outside the exhausted insect.

Finally it dropped off, leaving the cricket lifeless and shrunken. I had been present at the death of one of my meadow creatures and the birth into adulthood of another. For the thread was a "horsehair snake," or Gordian worm, which lives its young life as a parasite in insects and emerges as an adult to breed.

When I lived in Plymouth, Connecticut, we had an old horse-watering fountain in the center of town. We used to find the worms in the bottom of it. "Horsehairs that turned into worms," the town constable once told me. This was the common belief. Strange as such a belief was, it was no stranger than the facts of life of these creatures, whose ratio of length to thickness may be 1000:1 and whose bodies sometimes may be three feet long.

Such are just a few of the teeming residents of my meadow. Beneath its surface the moles tunnel endlessly for earthworms, sometimes maiming them to prevent escape and storing them in underground vaults like winter apples. In its soil are countless beetle grubs, roundworms, protozoans, the little honeypots of the bumblebees and the paper palaces of the yellow-jacket wasps. Above its surface dance clouds of insects, laced in and out with the sweep of swallows, the flash of flycatchers. Goldfinches feed on its dandelion fluff and thistledown, turtles nibble its wild strawberries, blacksnakes follow its mice into their burrows.

Yet, like a man in an airplane who sees nothing moving on the earth below, we may overlook it all. I recall one morning as I sat with a friend at the edge of a field following a sunrise hike.

"Do you see anything?" he asked as I scanned the meadow through my binoculars.

"No," I replied without thinking, "there's nothing in that meadow. Nothing at all."

I must have been back in my airplane.

AUTUMN

CHAPTER THIRTEEN

Goose Summer

THE FIRST FLYING cater-
pillars I can remember hatched out on my windowsill. I was
in second grade. As a school project, we were clipping egg
masses from fruit trees. Then we burned them. My sister
clipped and burned faithfully, but my brother and I weren't
so meticulous. After we'd collected a paper bag full, we pro-
ceeded to forget them.

When I remembered them several days later, they were eggs
no longer. Hatching out in the warm room, they were now
tiny hungry caterpillars. They laid down silken strands as they

searched for the new green apple-leaves that were supposed to be waiting for them.

I carried the bag out with its living cargo. A breeze was blowing as I stepped outside. It caught at the silk. Soon it had loosened several strands. A caterpillar, still clinging to its silk, was wafted into the air. Others followed, one by one, as I watched.

The little insects, weak from lack of food, were being carried to new fields by a kindly breeze. However, there was little hope for them: it was mid-February.

My next flying caterpillars came years later. As I sat in my lawn chair one balmy morning, I watched them go slowly by. They were newly hatched gypsy-moth larvae. They hung from a silk thread which streamed vertically into the air, caught by updrafts. The tiny mites of insect life at their lower ends dangled like marionettes on a string. They drifted across the lawn and out over the meadow.

Since then I've discovered that flying caterpillars are not uncommon. Paying out enough silk as the breeze pulls it from their mouths, many little potential cocoon-spinners are off for a ride.

One August day, however, I witnessed a silken airlift far greater than any I had ever seen. This time it was not caterpillars, but spiders. We were out picking wild raspberries in the north pasture. Just as I reached for a berry, I noted a tiny spiderling perched on it. Its body tilted skyward as the breeze drew out its silk. It raised up on its eight legs like a little toe dancer.

The moment of freedom came. The little creature sailed away. As my eyes followed it into the sky, I was dazzled by a luminous glow. The air shimmered as I'd never seen it do before.

The tiny spider was but one of countless thousands—perhaps millions—of its kind abroad that afternoon. The sun caught their delicate webs and highlighted them, just as dust motes glow in the light of a sunbeam. Some were just pinpoints drifting perhaps hundreds of feet above me. Others, closer, were vertical streaks of radiance. One, caught in an unlucky downdraft, crashed but a few inches from the point her cousin had vacated a moment before.

"Goose summer," my grandmother used to call such early fall days when the gossamer threads filled the air. These little spiders were the product of a season's work by their mothers. Now they were utilizing the highway provided by the air for the spread of their species.

Some would go only a few feet. Some would go miles. The grandparents of my little raspberry tenant might have lived on the next farm or in the next state. Baby spiders have been found on top of the Himalayas. They've been reported by ships at sea. They've been found in air-samples taken by rockets a dozen miles above the earth's surface. Going into something like suspended animation in the cold of upper air, they may drift for weeks before coming to earth far from their native land.

As we stopped to admire the late-summer air with its glistening burden, we saw it at work in another way. Out in the meadow danced a "dust devil." It whirled around, catching sticks, grass and leaves in an ascending spiral, carrying them some fifty feet in the air. Then the devil lost its identity and collapsed. Magnified a thousandfold, this harmless little updraft could have been a howling tornado, shattering houses and trees and sometimes carrying objects for long distances. Beetles, ants and even grasshoppers have been found on mountain snowfields, probably whipped there by some freakish updraft.

One team of scientists flew an airplane with flypaper on its

113

wings over a measured area in Louisiana. On the basis of such studies it's been figured that there may be 25 million insects and other small creatures in a single square mile of space. Oddly enough, those found highest were not necessarily the strongest flyers. Many were weak, feeble creatures such as aphids. Some, like the worker ants, were completely wingless. Lacking strong power of flight, they could not make their way to earth again.

"What do they mean—empty air?" asked Tom one day. We were looking at a sample of autumn haze through our home microscope. We had collected it by exposing a sticky glass plate to the air for twenty-four hours.

"There's a whole bunch of round things that must be pollen grains," my son continued. "Here's some green—it must be algae. And what's this? It looks like a little mite." He went on talking to himself as he squinted through the eyepiece.

We found bits of lichen, mold spores, airborne seeds, and a number of bedraggled insects on our sticky plate. Like the spiders and caterpillars, they had been seeking new fields over the aerial highway.

Ants, they say, have a perfect sense of timing—they are never late to a picnic. But an even greater finesse is shown by the worker ants' winged brothers and sisters. They may burst out of a score of anthills at once.

During the season, new winged squadrons have been developing in the underground nests. These are the flying reproductive individuals which are to be the nucleus of new ant colonies. The huge humpbacked females and their smaller prospective mates pay no attention to each other in the ground, but constantly wander toward the entrance to the hole. There they are firmly blocked by the workers. They cannot just fly away at any time. The day of emergence must be exactly right.

Finally, conditions are perfect. Temperature, moisture, barometric pressure are ideal. Sometimes this is just before or after a rain, but often it's on a sunny day. Somehow all the nests of the species get the signal at the same time. The myriads of winged ants rush out, surrounded and attended by milling workers.

They climbed hurriedly toward the light. In seconds the grass blades and weeds are alive with them. Each one seeks a take-off point. As it reaches the tip of the grass and launches into the air, another takes its place, and so on. From a hundred nests in the meadow, the rising thousands of flying ants make wisps like little columns of smoke.

At such times the insect-eaters have a feast. I remember a nest of little brown ants on my back lawn which sent out its reproductives to seek their fortunes. However, a garden toad had been tipped off. He sat to one side and snapped them up until his sides bulged.

But nature had the last word. In a careless moment he sat on the nest itself. Instantly he was covered with dozens of potential snacks. In his frantic efforts to be rid of their crawling he tumbled over backward and lost sight of the nest. The stream of little aviators, previously detoured into this gulping dead-end, took the main trail once more. Within seconds they were mingling with others in the air.

The ant drone soon dies after mating. The ant princess, now a potential queen, drops to earth. Now she seeks to avoid the light which formerly called her. The wings will be useless underground; she breaks them off. Then she flees from sight.

In a tiny chamber she lays a few eggs. Nourished by absorbing her own wing-muscles, she can find no food for the ant grubs. She feeds them with her saliva. The first grubs to emerge may be fed on the yet unhatched eggs. Under such conditions of near-starvation the first brood is produced. Its members are small and stunted. They take care of the nest from then on.

It's easy to find a newly mated queen and watch her prepare for household duties, for the queens flutter down from the sky in hundreds. Putting one in a narrow aspirin bottle covered with black paper, I find that she's made her little chamber the next day.

With some species, entomologists say, you'll find a worker clinging to the queen on her maiden flight—even going down into the ground with her to be ready to help with the chores at once. Some ants grow fungus as food in underground gardens. The queen may tuck a bit of fungus under her chin before her honeymoon, like a little trousseau. Then she can use it to start a little garden of her own.

Insects are not the only travelers in the autumn air. Each season thousands of people suffer from hay fever. "I hate to see the goldenrod blossom," they say. "Its darned pollen gives me the sniffles every year."

The real offender, of course, is a less-conspicuous pollinator, the ragweed. Goldenrod pollen is often heavy, chunky and clumped together. It travels only a few feet. Ragweed, however, blooming at the same time, produces high-flying pollen. It scatters like dust. I don't happen to get hay fever, but a good sniff of the greenish blossoms of ragweed will make me sneeze as if it were a handful of pepper.

No two species of plant pollen, supposedly, are the same. We agree, after sampling the living air with our sticky glass plate. We've seen three-cornered pollen, square pollen, six-sided, fourteen-sided. There is pollen with pits, bumps, spines, ridges, grooves. Some pollen grains are round, others are flat and disclike, others convex, concave, long, short, spiral. But all serve the primary purpose of reproduction laid down for them perhaps 200 million years ago as the seed plants developed.

"Prairie smoke," the people of our Midwest call them. These are the thousands of airborne seeds of South Dakota's state flower, the pasque flower. This little plant, *Anemone patens,* doesn't grow as far east as Vermont. However, I've seen Green Mountain smoke. In fact, a group of us once thought we were seeing flying saucers to boot.

The "smoke" is the sudden release of feathery seeds from thistles or goldenrod as the wind catches them. Our flying saucers were the seed-balloons of milkweed, caught up into the air and dancing in the sunlight before our incredulous eyes. Not realizing how near they really were, we mistakenly believed them to be miles high in the atmosphere. Just as we were wondering whether we'd had too much sun or whether we'd better call the nearest airport, another gust of wind caught some milkweed seeds close by. They rose and joined the others, thus squelching a scare story in tomorrow's newspaper before it was written.

Once I read somewhere that the average person seldom raises his eyes more than 15 degrees above his own horizon. Thus most of us go around beneath what we regard as a vast, flat inverted cone of nothingness.

But not because there's nothing there. Intent on our own berry-picking, lawnmowing or TV-viewing, we never take the opportunity to discover the secrets of life in the air above us.

CHAPTER FOURTEEN

Fall Fashions

WHEN I was small, I used to think that autumn came with the first frost. Later our teacher told us in grammar school that it arrives on September 21. For millions of vacationists and resort owners it begins the day after Labor Day.

For my trees and shrubs, however, autumn may come in April. Lured into early growth by an unusually warm series of days, they may set new green leaves before spring is fully established. Then one night the air becomes clear and still. Even the spring peepers, who often sing in water which still contains

119

melting ice, fall silent. The stars crackle down as bright as on a winter night.

In the morning the land is coated with frost. My bird feeder becomes populous once more, as song sparrows, chickadees and nuthatches find birdseed and suet easier picking than the numb insects which have fallen to the ground.

When the frost goes, the trees present a sorry sight. Their spring-green foliage is black and withered. In a couple of weeks, however, there are once again new leaves on the trees.

Fortunately, even in the rush of new growth in April, they had heeded some unspoken warning. Even as those first ill-fated little leaves were bursting out, tiny new buds were being formed. If the seasons behaved as they should, those buds would lie, unused, along the stem at the base of the leaves. Then when the leaves dropped, they would be ready for next year.

Now, however, they were nature's valuable ace-in-the-hole. Triggered by this quick autumn-and-winter all rolled into one night, they are ready for growth when spring comes again. This may be that very afternoon. Within a couple of weeks many of the scars of the freeze have healed, and the land is green once more.

I have found this safety-belt provision of nature in many of the lives around me, both plant and animal. If I trim my asparagus plants of their single spears, new ones come out of the ground in their place. A one-legged woodpecker learned to use his wings for balance as he whacked away at the dead stubs in our sugar maples. A raspberry cane at the edge of my garden was half buried by a clod of soil, but it merely put out new roots at that point and became a new plant. Once I found a crayfish, that little fresh-water lobster, which had lost an eye.

Since eyes are outgrowths of the brain and hence irreplaceable, the crayfish had found an admirable substitute. It had produced an extra antenna at that point. This sensitive organ of feeling was probably the next best thing to an eye that the crayfish could manage.

I didn't realize for some time that the annual shedding of leaves might also be a safety-belt. Yet it is, of course. That broad leaf area would not only be useless to a tree in winter, it would be a definite handicap. A full-sized elm may have nearly seven million leaves, each with thousands of pores through which moisture may be lost to the air. In winter, the drying effect of harsh winds is enormously reduced if these leaves are discarded.

I saw the same defensive measure in the Southwest in summer. Desert plants, faced with a severe drought, dropped their leaves. Remaining behind were the bare stems and tiny buds, waiting for better conditions.

"Jack Frost," says an old book on my shelf, "arrives in the fall and paints the leaves of the trees with little rainbows." However, the colors are not the direct result of his work. In college we extracted carotene, a carrot-colored pigment, from a normal-appearing green leaf. It had been there all the time, but masked by the green of the chlorophyll. In other leaves which were beginning to lose their chlorophyll, we found more of the anthocyanins, which supply the reds and purples.

"The fall colors are formed in this way," said our professor. "During the growing season, chlorophyll is manufactured almost constantly in the presence of light. The yellow and orange pigments, though they may be present, do not show through the green. Then, as the season goes on, less chlorophyll is manufactured. The yellow shows through. In other leaves, anthocyanins are produced, especially toward the end of the growing season. Couple this with the loss of chlorophyll and you have a red leaf."

Leaves fall to the ground, he told us, because of a layer of corky substance which forms at the base of each leaf. When it gets thick enough, the leaf no longer receives moisture from the branch. As it falls, the corky layer left behind forms a scab which covers the wound. Thus the tree doesn't lose its sap through a million leaf-scars—another safety measure provided by nature.

There's a horse-chestnut tree on a neighbor's lawn near my house. One October it split off a limb in a storm. As I helped clean up the debris, the resin from its huge buds made sticky spots on my hands and clothes. This, too, was part of a winter wardrobe. Shedding water, the resin prevented moisture from getting inside the bud scales.

I pulled a bud apart with my fingers; it was packed with cottony insulation around its tender growing-point. While some buds snuggle against the twig for protection, those of the horse chestnut spring out, large and bold, but shielded, nonetheless, inside and out.

Heavy scales, resin rainwear, fuzzy overcoats, half-hidden buds—these and more are provisions against winter by the woody plants. The herbs, like grass and clover and chickweed, die back to the soil. There the roots lie dormant, safe against winter chill.

But of course it's not only plants that prepare for cold weather ahead.

"I thought you said that every bird could be told by its color," Peg accused me one September afternoon as she handed me the binoculars. "What do you make of *that* bird?"

I squinted at it. About all I could tell of the color was that it didn't have much. It was olive-yellow with a little gray here and there. "Some kind of warbler," I grinned, "in his fall coat."

That's about all we've been able to say about many of the birds we meet on our fall walks. With no more need for a smart mating outfit to impress the ladies, most of the male birds don a somber suit. Their mates and children are equally conservative in dress.

These are their traveling clothes. They wear them south for the winter. For some reason, though, most of the birds that stay with us all year round make little change in appearance at any season. Our black-eyed little chickadees look about the same in January as they do in June. So do the sparrows, the woodpeckers and the nuthatches.

Beneath the homespun of these year-rounders, however, there is often a suit of winter underwear. Tom and I found it on a ruffed grouse which had flown into the side of a cabin. As it lay in our hands, momentarily dazed, we parted its feathers to make sure that no skin had been broken. At the base of many of the feathers were little downy tufts. What cold happened to get through the outer layer would be effectively trapped in this layer of fluff.

One autumn evening we were seated around the supper table. It was rather late in the day and the sun was below the hill. During a lull in the conversation, we became aware of a scampering on the front porch.

"Chipmunk," predicted Roger as we tiptoed to the window. "I bet he's after our apples."

We looked out at the box of McIntoshes, but there was no little striped creature helping himself. As we stood there wondering, there was a thump on the floor.

"My chicken!" gasped Peg.

She'd taken a package of fowl from the freezer and put it

on the little porch table to thaw for tomorrow's meal. Now it was gone.

Still tiptoeing, we opened the door and looked out. The chicken lay on the floor, but there was not a sign of the thief. Peg brought in the package and I left the tip of a wing on the table.

The next day the wing was gone. I put out more. It, too, disappeared the following night. There was no clue as to our visitor. I knew one thing, however: it liked chicken.

Then one noon Peg came to the door of my study. "Dinner ready . . . ?" I began. But she motioned me to silence.

"Got a surprise for you on the front porch," she said.

I had tacked a raw bone to a board and laid it on the table. Then if our visitor returned, I hoped he'd have to make enough noise getting away with the bone so we could see what he was. But I hadn't dared hope to see him in broad daylight.

"There's your mystery," she said. "What is it?"

A creature about a foot long tugged at the bone. Its back was a gray-brown, its underparts a snowy white. Lean and low, it seemed scarcely larger around than a mouse.

"Well, I'll be darned—a weasel!" I murmured to the children.

I'd long ago learned to speak in a murmur. The sibilant sound of a whisper causes more consternation among wild creatures than a steady, low voice. A bird or chipmunk would not have noticed my low exclamation in the slightest.

This, however, was no bird or chipmunk. It was a highstrung bundle of nerves. I learned much about weasels in that next moment.

First, it had easily heard my voice. It looked up immediately.

Second, it knew I was more than just an indefinable hunk

124

of something at the window. It looked right into my eyes.

Third, it had a wicked set of teeth. It bared them at me in an audible hiss.

Fourth, it was amazingly strong. It gave one jerk at the bone and twisted it right off the board.

Fifth, it was incredibly swift. Bone and weasel sprang to the floor, then shot across the porch to a mousehole. There the bone stopped, but the weasel continued without a pause. Almost before I finished my ill-considered exclamation, it was gone.

Now that we had met, it became less secretive. We saw it daily for a week. We never failed to marvel at its precise movements. One day I put my camera to the window and clicked the shutter. In that instant, the weasel was gone. I had to wait until the film was developed to know whether I had a picture or not.

Then one day the meat was left untouched. "No more weasel," I told the children when a new piece was still there a second day. Hopefully, however, we kept the food out several days longer.

It was gone for nearly a month. Then we heard the scamper again. I put out fresh meat. The next day our weasel was back. But it was a weasel no more. It, too, had adopted the fall fashions. It was dressed in an immaculate coat of royal ermine.

The brown hairs had dropped out as the new ones grew in. Now it was ready for the winter snows, with only its dark eyes and black tail-tip to give it away.

Our ermine stayed with us for half a year more. Finally it disappeared. Possibly it got tired of tame hamburger and chicken, and went to seek livelier prey.

But if a hawk or an owl caught it, I know one thing. That

bird sure got its talons full.

"Going to be a hard winter," said a neighbor one day as we watched a squirrel in a beech tree. "Look at the thick fur on that squirrel's tail."

There are lots of ways we try to forecast what the coming winter will be. If my chipmunks retire early, it's supposed to be an ominous sign. So is heavy hair on a cow, or an extra-thick layer of fat on the back of a bear. If the fish in Lake Champlain strike for deep water early, they're trying to get away from the cold to come. "There's fur-bearing trout in Lake Memphremagog," one old-timer solemnly assures me. Early geese overhead and extra honey in the hive tell you to get out your long-handled underwear.

The most famous fur coat of all, however, is that of the woolly-bear caterpillar, *Isia isabella*. Over much of our continent, this little black-and-brown creature with a crew-cut hurries across roads and sidewalks in the fall. His black head and tail end are like the locomotive and caboose to the brown central portion of his body.

He ripples along as fast as he can. At a touch he curls up, but soon loses bashfulness and is again on the way. Weather prophets anxiously scan the markings on the woolly bear; the wider the central brown band, the browner (less snowy) the winter will be. Another group of weather seers, however, says just the opposite: a wide brown band means deep snow.

There happens to be one prophet of each kind in Lincoln. Every autumn they contradict each other over whole handfuls of woolly bears.

Their results are just what you'd expect. "See?" gloats one in the spring, "I told you it'd be a hard winter."

"Hmph!" says the other. "It ain't nearly as hard as it *could* have been."

CHAPTER FIFTEEN

Mushrooms, or ---?

W E BECAME acquainted with the Hubbells when a three-foot section of their lawn began to rise mysteriously in the air. They knew I was interested in natural history, so they got me on the telephone.

"There's something underneath it that's pushing it up," Bill Hubbell told me. "Could you come up and see what it is?"

This was just another of many strange requests I've had ever since I gained notoriety with a cage full of snakes in second grade. People call me to tell about their pet chipmunks, turtles and foxes. One day last year a carload of strangers rumbled

129

over our bridge to show me their squirtless skunk. And as soon as possible I'm to go to Addison to photograph a pet woodchuck.

I look forward to these requests. They add still more spice to my already zestful life here in the country. This, however, was the first time I'd been faced with a lawn that wouldn't stay put.

When I got there Bill took me out behind his house.

"See? That whole chunk of lawn is rising. What's causing it?"

Carefully we dug away at one edge of the green slab. Beneath it were dozens of white pillars. Each one looked like an elongated giant thimble, about four inches high.

"Mushrooms," I said in amazement. "Hundreds of them. They're coming up so thick that they're raising the grass in a sheet."

I took some home and checked them with my mushroom book. They were the "shaggy mane," a type which comes up in the fall in rich lawns and meadows. The next day I was back with a big paper bag.

"You're not going to *eat* those?" he asked. "How do you know they're not toadstools?"

This time I had the book with me. I showed him how they were related to *Coprinus,* the little brown tent-like mushrooms that grow at the base of old stumps. I had often eaten the little ones, and the book said the big shaggy manes were every bit as good.

He remained unconvinced. "Before I'd touch one of them, you'd have to prove they weren't poison."

Even as he spoke, I absent-mindedly popped one into my mouth. I chewed for a while as he gaped at me. Then I swallowed it before his incredulous eyes.

He swallowed hard, right along with me. Relishing the occasion, I held out one to him. "Want one? They're good."

Actually, mushrooms are as tasty raw as cooked. Peg sometimes sneaks a few into a fresh tossed salad for variety. But she usually has to do it when nobody's looking.

A great number of creatures eat quantities of mushrooms—raw, of course. Deer are fond of them. So are skunks. Once I cared for more than one hundred raccoons for a state wildlife department; they loved them, too. Mice, grouse, muskrats, woodchucks, foxes, insects, squirrels, centipedes, snails—nearly all my animal neighbors may meet around a mushroom table. Yet, with all these creatures as living proof of the wholesomeness of these fungus parasols, people are still skeptical. When we eat wild mushrooms we usually eat alone.

The trouble is that there is no infallible rule of thumb for picking out the dozen or so poisonous species from some hundred and fifty that are edible. "Put a silver spoon in the pot," goes an old fallacy; "if it stays shiny, a meal you've got." This is wrong on two counts. First, not all "toadstools," as poisonous mushrooms are often called, will tarnish silver. Second, some edible mushrooms will. So will eggs, for that matter.

Other rules say to pick only mushrooms which have pink gills, solid stems or grow on wood. Still others warn against a "death cup" at the base, a ring around the stem or a milky juice. For one reason or another, none of these rules is much better than the silver-spoon test. You can't even stake your fate on a sample of a suspicious one. One of the most poisonous of all is reported to be delicious to the taste.

"The safest way," said Louis Lake, a naturalist whom I worshiped as a boy, "is to be able to call the mushroom by name—both common and scientific. Get a book. Learn it well. That takes time, I know. But once you've learned a species you'll know it from then on as an old friend."

During the past twenty years or so, I've learned to recognize some three dozen such old friends. They range from the tiny coral mushrooms which hide in the gloom of my forest to the giant puffballs which appear like white bowling balls in my meadow. The former may weigh scarcely a tenth of an ounce, the latter ten pounds or more.

There is a mushroom which looks like a big piece of raw beefsteak—even to the red juice when it's cut. There is another which dissolves into an inky fluid overnight. Another turns blue when you break it; another oozes an orange liquid. Each of these sounds distinctive, and it is. But equally distinctive are most of the others once you get to know them. A friend of Tom's can call out the make and year of an approaching car almost before I can tell the color. Yet, as he said, "all those funguses are toadstools to me."

Most of our "funguses" make their way directly to the frying pan or table. Others get sidetracked to the freezer. We freeze them, all fried, until needed. Last year we put up twenty pounds of fried puffballs alone.

"If we pick these mushrooms, will more grow next year?" I once asked Mr. Lake. He assured me that they would. Mushrooms are just the fruiting bodies of vast underground networks of fungal strands called mycelium. Often the strands of a species are of two types, which might be termed *a* and *b*. When they meet, they send up a little button. This looks like a puffball at first, but if it is cut lengthwise, the future stem and cap will be seen.

"Picking mushrooms causes no more harm to the mycelium than picking apples does to the tree," he said.

"I always cut a puffball in half," he continued. "If it's one solid mass of mealy white, I know it's the real thing. But if it has a hidden stem and gills, I throw it away. The 'button stage' of mushrooms is too hard to identify."

The whole point of the above-ground mushroom is to produce spores. These will be the start of new generations. Each spore, dropping from the gills, drifts away on the air. Peg's Girl Scouts made spore prints one time by placing mushroom caps, gills down, on a piece of paper. The next day the thousands of tiny specks had fallen on the paper. They gave a marvelously symmetrical image of the gills above. They were in a number of colors, ranging from white through pink and brown to black.

As an experiment I tore up and threw around bits of mushrooms in the hope that spores from their caps would germinate. Then perhaps luck will bring together types *a* and *b* (or *c* and *d* in species with more than two types), and I'll have my own crop in a year or two. Since a healthy mushroom may discharge half a million spores a minute into the air, I imagine there's already a pretty steady rain of potential delicacies coming down on my hundred acres.

Mushrooms have another way of getting around.

Four years ago a friend and I stood at the edge of his brand-new lawn. Near its center was a ring of white mushrooms. They were scattered in a circle perhaps six feet in diameter.

"How did such a ring come about?" he puzzled.

We theorized that perhaps a bit of mycelium had come in with the topsoil brought in by a truck. Growing out in every direction, it had finally sent up the little mushrooms in this "fairy ring," as it is called.

"Seems to me," he added, "that the grass inside that ring is greener than that in the rest of the lawn. The mushrooms must be helping the grass to grow somehow."

We've watched it every year since that time. The ring has

nearly doubled in diameter annually. His thoughts about the grass were correct, too. Although the fairy ring doesn't appear until fall, we can pinpoint the unseen growth of the mycelium simply by observing the new ring of the lush green grass. I'm wondering, though, what will happen to the mushrooms when they march out beyond the lawn, under the sidewalk and into the street.

"Symbiosis," scientists call the close relationship between two living species, such as that between the mushrooms and the grass. In our fields and woods it can be of momentous importance.

Studies have unearthed roots of entire trees literally blanketed with underground fungal strands. Despite what would seem to be a smothering mass of mycelium, the trees were strong and healthy. Other studies have experimentally removed all fungus growth from the soil, and plants have done poorly. Some have refused to grow at all.

"These fungus roots, called mycorrhizae, enter into partnership with a great many plants," a soil biologist told a group of us at a farm meeting. "We don't know exactly how they do it, but somehow they help the plants get more out of every cubic inch of soil. When you consider that a seedling may get twice as much nitrogen, potassium and phosphorus from the same batch of soil, you can see how important mycorrhizal fungi can be."

When I was seven years old, I gave my wrist a bad gash on a scythe. My grandmother, who happened to be visiting at the time, stanched the bleeding. Then she bound a piece of moldy bread on the wound.

Grandma didn't know why she used moldy bread. "Moldy fruit skins are better," she told my mother as she dressed my wrist. This was in 1927—two years before Sir Alexander Fleming discovered penicillin. Its source, *Penicillium,* is a mold fungus—a powerful weapon for the doctor and a bane to the housewife.

Thus does a commonplace become achievement in the hands of the talented.

One fall afternoon we were sitting under the elms of a friend in Burlington. An old tree, long since a victim of disease, had been reduced to a tall stump. On its side grew whole shelves of delicious white "oyster" mushrooms.

"Would you mind if I took a bagful of those home with me?" I asked my hostess. "They're wonderful eating."

She looked startled. I could see the old fear of "toadstools" struggling in her mind with her friendship for me. "If it's all the same to you, Ron, I'd rather you didn't," she said.

Our conversation turned to other matters. After a while I left. I spent a few minutes shopping downtown. On my way home I again drove past her house.

She had set a stepladder against the tree, and was chopping away at the mushrooms with a hatchet. As they fell, her son stuffed them into a trash bucket.

This was flattery in a way, I guess. We were old friends. She wanted to be sure I'd be around for years to come.

CHAPTER SIXTEEN

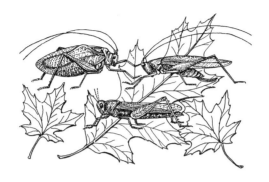

Grasshoppers' Farewell

WHEN I THINK of autumn, I recall one thing above all. While others see in their memories the flaming leaves and ripening fruit, and still others remember sunny goldenrod and blue-rayed asters, I am mindful of one sound which haunts these bittersweet days. That sound is the farewell of the grasshoppers.

In May they were silent. In June and July the sound was just a thin whisper. The only ones to sing were a few early maturing 'hoppers which had shed their last nymphal coats and become winged adults. But as the days wear on, their whisper gains volume. The sound increases as the grasshoppers' first cousins—often lumped in general terms as grasshoppers, too—join in the chorus. Crickets are often first, leaving their adolescence behind and proclaiming their maturity through the familiar chirp. They are joined by the long-horned grasshoppers, or false katydids, with their sibilant calls. Finally the insect orchestra is complete when the true katydid adds its measured bass.

"Frost in six weeks," Dad used to say when he heard the first katydid in the old cherry tree. But the long-legged green insect with the convex wings never seemed to care. It just went on, all through most of the night: "Ká-ty-did . . . ka-ty-did." Or, just, "She-did . . . she-did." We three children sometimes lay in our sleeping bags out under the tree and, remembering Dad's prediction, we imagined that the katydid intoned over and over, "Six-weeks . . . six-weeks."

We were seldom able to find the katydid in its treetop home, but we were more fortunate in our search for crickets. Now, each autumn, I relive my own boyhood days as I show my children how to find these black little songsters. In sneaking up on a cricket we stop when it stops, move forward as it sings again. We can speak all we wish, for the high-pitched little creature seems to be deaf to our comparatively low voices. Let us jar the earth, though, and the singer falls silent.

We like to catch the songster unaware. Somehow it seems as if we are sharing a great secret. Not only is he hard to find in his little grass-roots cave, but his singing appearance is quite unusual. Wings raised high, like a tiny black mother-hen defending her chicks, he announces his circle of territory to all other crickets. With each rasp of the wings, a chirp is produced. Ladies are welcome, but gentlemen appear at their own peril.

"It says here," Peg observed as she was reading the newspaper, "that an unmated female cricket will make her way to a loudspeaker which is playing a recording of a male's song. On the other hand, once a female has mated, she will no longer be attracted to the note of the male."

"Naturally," said I. "Fulfillment."

"Disillusionment," she corrected.

Entomologists call the grasshoppers and their relatives the most musical of all insects. But their sound is more of a buzz than a song. One time at a science fair a high-school sophomore pointed this out to me.

"Look under the microscope at this cricket wing," he directed. A saw-tooth section was in focus under the lens. "That's known as the file. There's one on each wing. That hardened area is known as a scraper. When the scraper on one wing rubs on the file of the other, the wings are thrown into vibration. That's the way the sound is produced.

"Many crickets can rub with either wing," he continued, "so they're ambidextrous. Most of our grasshoppers have a file on the left wing only. So they're left-handed."

All the long summer and autumn days and nights the insect chorus swells. It becomes a backdrop to everything we do. As we lie at night in the open meadow around the 12th of August to watch the Perseid shower of meteors, the musicians play about us. As the nights grow cooler their exuberance fades, only to be redoubled in the morning sun. Now there's no stopping them; we can almost touch a singing long-horned grasshopper or red-legged locust before it ceases. Once I saw a Carolina locust whose hopper-legs had been snatched away by some enemy. This species sings on the wing. Unable to spring into the air itself, it rattled and crackled gratefully when I tossed it skyward.

The sound of the insects becomes a tumult. "Good heavens!" Janice finally exclaimed one October afternoon as the air throbbed with sound, "how on earth can they hear themselves in all that noise?"

Perhaps each one is tuned to its own special frequency. On the other hand, some, like the female tree cricket, are apparently deaf, unless they feel vibrations through their feet or antennae. The ears of the other grasshoppers and katydids are in strange places. Katydid and cricket ears are on their front legs. Some grasshoppers wear theirs on each side of the abdomen.

We watched a tiny grasshopper on a ragweed as it fiddled intermittently with both hind legs, rubbing them on the outside of its wings. Carefully, I put my head close. I could just hear a slight rustling noise, but nothing that might be called a song. Yet another grasshopper ten feet away fiddled in exact timing with this one. He rubbed when it did, stopped when it stopped. All this went on in silence, as far as my ears could discover.

This gives point to an interesting fact. That riot of voices we hear on an autumn afternoon is probably just a disjointed fragment of an even greater sound, forever inaudible to our ears. A few of these voices get through, it is true. A beekeeper knows the sound of an angry bee as differing from that of a complacent one, for instance. In fact, a healthy bee sings "A" at 435 wing-vibrations per second, while the house fly hums "F" of the middle octave at 345 vibrations. But much, if not the majority, of the insect chorus is too high or too faint for us to hear.

Imperfectly heard as the sound may be to our ears, it is sufficient for the insects. They find their mates in the autumn heat. Buzzing furiously in the sun, they chase each other around stems and through the grass. They sing and fly and mate in an orgy that continues day after day.

I can recall catching a mating pair of grasshoppers and putting them into a bait can for an afternoon's fishing. When I got to the pond, they were still locked together.

The mated female, like the mated cricket, shows little further interest in romance. Now the foundation must be laid for next year's insect chorus. In spite of the Aesop fable, she lays up a winter store.

We watched one as she went about the task. Prodding with the sharp prongs at the end of her abdomen, she sampled the sun-baked dirt. Finally she found a spot to her liking and bored down through it. Her abdominal segments telescoped out until she was half again her normal length.

We could see her strain as the eggs were forced into their cradle an inch below the surface. Later we dug them up. There were about fifty—long and white, like little sausages.

Sometimes one of the plants breaks over in the garden. We examine the break. Often we find long rows of other eggs in the central pith. They were introduced, hypodermic-needle fashion, by the sharp ovipositors of crickets and katydids.

The chorus continues, cheerful as ever, loud as ever. Then one day the Burlington radio strikes an ominous note.

"Fair today, but with sharply lowering temperatures after sundown," the announcer warns. "Danger of frost in the higher elevations."

I turn off the radio. Then the children and I walk out through the meadow. Our progress is marked by a moving island of silence in a sea of sound, as the startled insects cut short their songs and jump out of the way.

"Will they all die tonight?"

"No, Roger. When the cold comes, they lose their hold and

drop down among the grass roots where it's warm."

He and Alison caught as many as they could and put them in a big jar. "Just 'til morning, Dad. Then we'll let them out again."

That night I listen to the insects as they fall silent. Slower and slower come the calls of the tree crickets. Before the temperature drops to 50 degrees they cease entirely. By the time it's 45 on the thermometer, only a few hidden field crickets are still chirping. As I go to sleep I think of the katy-dids at our old home in Connecticut: "Ka——ty——did . . . . She——did."

The next morning, though the chorus has stumbled, it has caught itself, and goes on. It may continue for another three or four weeks. But then at last the knell is sounded. One morning we waken to see the fields white with rime. Jack's dish of water is covered with a solid layer of ice. Not a single musician of my insect chorus can be heard.

They lie, blackened and still, at the grass roots. Their lives are finished.

But underneath the soil, in the stems and beneath the bark, the eggs of the grasshoppers wait. They will burst to joyful life next spring when once again the land will come alive.

INDEX